AmaZing
AFRICA

Other books by Michael Nathan-Pepple:

1. ALL ABOUT ANTIGUA AND BARBUDA
Discover the history and heritage of this twin island nation, through some of its top sites and attractions.

2. HISTORICAL CHURCHES OF THE CARIBBEAN ISLAND OF ANTIGUA
An overview of the complex relationship between the older established churches, slavery and their black converts.

The books listed above are available on Amazon in both paperback and ebook formats.

AmaZing
AFRICA

Changing the narrative by
telling the African story

MICHAEL NATHAN-PEPPLE

MNP PUBLICATIONS
LONDON

Copyright © 2024 Michael Nathan-Pepple
Published by Michael Nathan-Pepple
For enquiries email: mnathanpepple@gmail.com

The right of the author to be identified as the Author of this Work have been asserted in accordance with the Copyright, Designs and Patents Act 1988.

All rights reserved. No part of this publication may be reproduced, stored in a retrieval system or transmitted, in any forms or by any means, electronic, mechanical, photocopying or otherwise, without the prior permission of the publisher.

ISBN: 978-1-9162807-2-4

DEDICATION

Dedicated to my beloved children Michael, Melissa, Matthew and Marcus, as well as my grandchildren Mya, Maurico and Zekhi.

SANKOFA

The above picture is an abstract illustration of Sankofa, a symbol used by the Akan-speaking people of Ghana. The symbol exemplifies the importance of reflecting and reclaiming one's traditional cultural values, in order to advance and move forward. It can also be simplified as 'Looking backwards to go forward.'

ANCESTRAL CALL!

Our Ancestors, both known and unknown. We need your help to revive our culture and heritage. Many Africans and African descendants around the world have historically been misled by Europeans and their ideals. They want us to believe that becoming western or living a western lifestyle is synonymous with progress and modernity.

These *deceitful exploiters* who have stolen from Africa and its people for centuries, would prefer that we look westward rather than inward. We must remember that Ancient Africa was aspirational and advanced, particularly in the areas of trade, medicine, agriculture and astronomy. To make any meaningful progress at this time, we must first reconnect with our African heritage (Sankofa) and invest in our culture.

Anyone of African descent who denies their African ancestry must admit that their history is short and began with slavery. Those who wish to reconnect with their African roots, on the other hand, will have thousands of years of history to embrace.

Michael Nathan-Pepple - Recalled from a dream on the morning of February 14, 2022.

"To know yourself,
you have to go back to your Roots"

CONTENTS

List of Illustrations 1
Acknowledgments 3
Foreword 4
Introduction 7

Chapter 1
Africa 11

Chapter 2
A to Z Characters from Africa 25

Chapter 3
Conclusion 71
The way forward for Africa 73

African Proverbs: Wisdom from Africa 79
Inspirational African proverbs
and their meaning 80

Glossary 82
Bibliography 84
Recommended reading 92

LIST OF ILLUSTRATIONS

1. African map showing its 54 countries 6
2. Wall painting in the tomb of Sarenput II 16
3. The Great Sphinx, with the pyramid of Khafre......... 16
4. Gold five guinea coins 16
5. Benin Bronzes.. 19
6. African colonies after the Berlin conference
   of 1884-5 22
7. Collage 1 48
   - *The mighty Africa Baobab tree*
   - *Cowrie shells on mask*
   - *Catalan Atlas, ca. 1375, showing Mansa Musa holding a giant gold nugget*
   - *The majestic African lion*
8. Collage 2 57
   - *Lemurs of Madagascar*
   - *Oware Board Game*
   - *The soul and spirit of the Asante nation lives in the Golding Stool*
   - *A section of the ruins of Great Zimbabwe*
9. Collage 3 70
   - *Saharan rock painting*
   - *Vintage Nigerian stamp honouring Queen Amina of Zaria*
   - *Rhinos at a game park in Southern Africa*
   - *African Zulu Warrior*

ACKNOWLEDGMENTS

This is my third book since deciding to pursue writing as a career, and I would like to appreciate my wife Sheralyn for her support and patience throughout. I thank her for serving as my main proof-reader from the book's inception to its publication. Other people who proof-read the book at various stages of its development included my son Michael Jnr, Fred Oshodi, an old family friend and brother, Pauline Williams, Aikigbe Alli, and a dear friend of my wife and I, Dr. Radcliffe Robins, who was very thorough, provided constructive criticism and encouraged me to write about Alkebulan.

When I asked Dr. Robins to write the book's foreword, he did not hesitate. In fact, he thanked me for the opportunity to do so. The Foreword conveys the essence of the book. Also, a big shout out to my friends and family members who encouraged me when I mentioned that I was going to write the book. Finally, I would like to thank the Most High Creator and all of my known and unknown ancestors for inspiring me to make this happen. Remember that Africa is the reason why everything exists.

FOREWORD

In the spirit of the poem *Still I Rise* by the distinguished poet Maya Angelou, Africa is marching today with majesty, to assert and ascertain her rightful place in human civilization and development:

> You may write me down in history
> With your bitter, twisted lies,
> You may trod me in the very dirt
> But still, like dust, I'll rise.

Africa has been written down in history with many deliberate, bitter and twisted lies, but beyond doubt there has been a tectonic shift in Africa's trajectory. It is a self-movement and a self-realisation that this time will be difficult to stop. This self-realisation has many signposts and highlights; I list three for your consideration: the defeat of apartheid in South Africa (June 1991), the declaration by the African Union (May 2012) that the African Diaspora is its 6th Region and the emergence of real post (neo) colonial independence and sovereignty as shown by the formation (September 2023) of the Alliance of Sahel states (Burkina Faso, Niger and Mali).

This shift is a re-statement by Africans of the African position; the retelling of *ourstory* from the perspective of our own eyes, history and ancestral experiences. Not from the perspective of the twisted lies and sanitised perspective of the coloniser.

The book AmaZing Africa is an example of this retelling. It illuminates Africa's past, the birth place of the human species, the cradle of human civilisation, Africa's contribution to political and social organisation, culture, metallurgy, agriculture and trade. It also delves into Africa's vast iconography and shares with us selections of this resource that immediately impact the human psyche or is unique to the African experience.

Finally AmaZing Africa explores the question of what is to be done. What are the necessary political, economic, cultural and individual changes that are required to assert African sovereignty and independence, freed from external domination, greed and control? The path to that solution may not be fully illuminated but it is sufficiently well lit. Sankofa will guide. Let the examination of Africa's ancestral knowledge and the vital lessons of its historical experience guide future actions.

> Leaving behind nights of terror and fear
> I rise
> Into a daybreak that's wondrously clear
> I rise
> Bringing the gifts that my ancestors gave,
> I am the dream and the hope of the slave.
> I rise
> I rise
> I rise.

AmaZing Africa Rises.

Dr. Radcliffe Robins

1. African map showing its 54 countries

INTRODUCTION

"The day will come when history will speak...
Africa will write its own history...
It will be a history of glory and dignity."

- PATRICE EMERY LUMUMBA (1925-1961)

AmaZing Africa was inspired by my children, who, as teenagers, were eager to learn more about Africa. The motivation for writing this book is to raise awareness of Africa and provide an insight into aspects of its exceptional history, unique cultures and dynamic heritage, while also rejecting many stereotypes about Africa and Africans. Many of these labels, such as the belief that Africans were savages, uncivilised, devoid of religions, unintelligent, lazy and dangerous, began with the institution of slavery and were later used to justify the European invasion and colonisation of Africa. Regrettably, these destructive narratives based on a lack of knowledge, misinformation, misrepresentation, white supremacy and racism, continue to shape how Africans and their descendants are perceived and treated all over the world.

Fortunately, communication (including the use of social media outlets) has become much easier around the world and people are learning to appreciate different cultures. The rise in cultural awareness is promoting a greater understanding among the human family, emphasising that today's world was shaped by the contributions of a much broader range of peoples and cultures.

Interestingly, some of what is referred to as Western knowledge comes from African and other indigenous civilisations that have existed around the world. Learning about these influences on human development contributes to a more complete and accurate picture of world history, paving the way for a more peaceful world free of racial and ethnic prejudice.

AmaZing Africa is specifically aimed at today's youth, regardless of ethnicity, as well as anyone interested in learning more about Africa's rich history, culture and heritage. The book contains not only factual information about Africa, but also features several key characters from the continent, such as the drum, cowrie shell, family, herbalist, xylophone and some animals unique to Africa. It also provides some relevant and useful information about each character chosen to support the African story, which could serve as a starting point for future research. Africans in Africa, the diaspora and the rest of the world must recognise and value Africa's contribution to human development. The book is titled AmaZing Africa because Africa is truly amazing. By changing the narrative, Africans could indeed begin to tell their own stories. In the words of the former African Union Ambassador to the United States, Ambassador Arikana Chihombori-Quao: "Africa is an amazing continent and everything you have heard or read negative about Africa is all false. Take another look at Africa with a clean eye."

Despite the brutality and unforgettable scars of the Trans-Saharan Slave Trade, aka the Arab Slave Trade (c.650-1900s), the Indian Ocean Slave Trade (c.800-1900s), the Trans-Atlantic Slave Trade, aka the

INTRODUCTION

Euro-American Slave Trade (c.1441-1888), and the subsequent era of European colonisation of the African continent (c.1885-1960s/70s), Africa's influence continues to resonate with people all over the world. More specifically, millions of African-descendants who were denied knowledge of their cultural identity and now reside in the Americas, Caribbean, Australia, Asia, and Europe are reconnecting with and celebrating their African heritage. These children of Africa, popularly referred to as the *African Diaspora*, have been officially recognised by the African Union as its 6th region. The African Union defines this region as "consisting of people of African origin living outside the continent, irrespective of their citizenship and nationality..." Therefore, to be an African goes beyond simply being born in Africa, as was eloquently put by Dr Kwame Nkrumah (First President of the Republic of Ghana and a principal icon of Pan-Africanism), "I am not African because I was born in Africa, but because Africa was born in me."

Chapter 1

AFRICA

Africa is widely recognised by historians and anthropologists as the birthplace of humanity or the Cradle of humankind. It is known as the *Mother Continent* because "three well-preserved skulls belonging to the earliest members of our own species, Homo sapiens [modern man]," (Connor, 2003) were discovered there. The fossil remains of these human ancestors are believed to be 160,000 years old. This acknowledges Africa as the spark that ignited civilisation and played a critical role in early human evolutionary history. During those ancient times, Africans across the continent moved from one stage of development to the next. They were responsible for domesticating a wide variety of plants and animals for food and other purposes. Domesticated animals included donkeys, guinea fowl and cattle, along with millet, coffee, yam, tamarind, watermelon, black-eyed peas, okra and hundreds of other plant species. Africa is home to numerous nations, ethnic groups and social groups, which may help to explain its reputation as the world's most culturally, linguistically and genetically diverse continent. It is surrounded by the Mediterranean Sea, the Red Sea, the Indian Ocean and the Atlantic Ocean, and its landscape is varied and beautiful, with vast highlands, lush rainforests, sprawling deserts and grasslands and pristine coastlines. The equator almost perfectly divides Africa in half.

Africa is the world's second-largest continent, with a population of approximately 1.4 billion people (equivalent of 18% of the total global population). It encompasses 30, 365,000 square kilometres (11,700,000 square miles), or 20% of the world's land area. Many Western countries continue to spread the myth that Africa is at risk of overpopulation. However, given Africa's abundant land, the idea of overpopulation seems absurd. In fact, Africa is large enough to accommodate the United States, China, India, Japan, Mexico and many European countries. Asia has the highest population density, followed by Africa and Europe. As a result, it is unclear why Western population experts continue to fund Non-Governmental Organisations (NGOs) and governments to slow Africa's population growth. In a newspaper article about global population issues, the author questioned why population reduction was always aimed at Africa, and whether it was due to the continent's lack of resources to feed its citizens. He concluded that Africa has a lot of resources and questioned whether this was because "some other countries want those resources for their own people instead" (Koutonin, 2016). Ironically, several European countries are encouraging families to have more children in order to boost their declining birth rate through cash incentives, tax breaks and loan forgiveness, whereas China, with roughly the same population as the entire African continent, has abandoned its one-child policy.

ANCIENT & HISTORICAL (PRE-COLONIAL) AFRICA

The history of Africa reveals notable achievements such as the founding of great civilizations, empires and kingdoms. Several of these nations, including the empires of Mutapa (Zimbabwe and

CHAPTER 1

Mozambique) and Axum (Eritrea and northern Ethiopia), as well as the kingdom of Kongo (parts of Angola, the Democratic Republic of Congo [DRC] and the Republic of Congo), Buganda (Uganda), Zulu (South Africa) and Benin (Nigeria), were large and powerful, with centralised political systems, complex infrastructures and extensive trade routes. Many of these civilisations existed long before Europeans arrived in Africa, exposing the deception and false narrative spread by countless *intellectual* Europeans who claimed Africa had no history.

Georg Hegel, a German philosopher, was one such person, whose 1899 book *The Philosophy of History* reinforced the Eurocentric racist 19th century belief that Africa had no past or history (Andindilile, 2016). This narrative was also echoed by Arthur Newton, former professor of Imperial History at King's College London, who claimed in the 1920s that Africa had "no history before the coming of the Europeans," (Watterson, 2008), and by the highly celebrated British historian Hugh Trevor-Roper in the 1960s, who stated, "perhaps, in the future; there will be some African history to teach. But at present, there is none. There is only the history of Europeans in Africa, the rest is largely darkness...and darkness is not a subject of history" (Msindo, 2019). On a visit to Senegal in 2007, former French President Nicolas Sarkozy echoed Hegel's sentiments, stating, "The tragedy of Africa is that the African has not fully entered into history...They have never really launched themselves into the future" (Ba, 2007).

During the pre-colonial era, kingdoms and empires dominated a large part of Africa, but there were also *stateless societies* with basic political and economic systems and no central authority, such as the Baule (Ivory Coast), Igbo (Nigeria), Dogon (Mali), Kru (Liberia), Maasai (Kenya & Tanzania), Kikuyu (Kenya), Khoi-San (southern

Africa), Karamojong (Uganda), Somali (Somalia) and Tiv (Nigeria). One of Africa's earliest and most ancient civilisations was that of Kemet (aka ancient Egypt), which emerged in the Nile Valley region over 5000 years ago. According to Dr. Cheick Anta Diop, a well-known Senegalese historian, Professor Theophile Obenga of Congo, Dr. Chancellor Williams, Dr. Ben Jochanan, John Herike Clark, Dr. Molefi Kete Asante and many other African and African-American scholars, Kemet was an indigenous African civilisation founded by Africans in Africa. However, there has been much debate about the ethnicity of ancient Egyptians, specifically whether they were Black Africans. Unfortunately, many people refuse to acknowledge that black people were capable of creating such a highly developed civilisation, due to racial stereotypes or complete ignorance.

In 2017, for example, in what was described as a *breakthrough* in DNA sequencing of Egyptian mummies, a team of German researchers revealed that ancient Egyptians were most closely related to people from the Near East, particularly the Levant region (present-day Jordan, Lebanon, Palestine/Israel, Syria and Turkey), as well as populations from Europe, rather than modern Egyptians and Africans south of the Sahara (Schuenemann, 2017). Interestingly, the mummified samples tested were carbon dated between the late New Kingdom and the Roman Period (1388 BCE-426 CE), implying that the study overlooked nearly 4,000 years of history, from pre-dynastic Egypt to the Middle Kingdom (2134-1690 BCE). It is worth noting that ancient Egypt was invaded or conquered by a number of foreign powers throughout its history, including the Hyksos (1658 BCE), Assyrians (671 BCE), Persians (525 BCE), Greeks (332), Romans (31 BCE) and Arabs (639 CE). This may explain why the population's complexion has gotten lighter over time. Furthermore, the area from which these samples were collected was too small in comparison to the total size of ancient Egypt. The researchers acknowledged this limitation, noting that "all of our genetic data were obtained from a single site in Middle Egypt and may not be representative for all of ancient Egypt." They went on to say that "the genetic makeup of the people in southern Egypt may have been different, being closer to the interior of the continent" (Perry, 2022).

In fact, two European historical figures, Herodotus (c. 454 BCE), a Greek historian and geographer, and Constantin-François Chasseboeuf, aka Count de Volney (1783-85 CE), a French historian, who visited Egypt at different times in history, described the ancient Egyptians as having dark skin, curly/woolly hair and the true face of a molatto. After seeing the Sphinx and noting its distinct Negroid features, Count Volney concluded that "the ancient Egyptians were real negroes [blacks], of the same species with all the natives of Africa" (Volney, 1787). He went on to say that, despite having mixed with the Greeks and Romans for many generations, they still bear a striking resemblance to their ancient ancestors (i.e. swollen faces, puffy eyes, flattened noses and thick lips). Furthermore, during his archaeological expedition to Egypt in 1828, the French historian and Egyptian hieroglyph decipherer Jean-Francois Champollion came to the same conclusion, stating that "the ancient Egyptians belonged to a race quite similar to the Kennous or Barabras, present inhabitants of Nubia [black Africans]" (Diop, 1974). Other ancient writers of antiquity who described ancient Egyptians with dark complexions or black skins included Aristotle, Achilles Tatius, Lucian of Samosata, Heliodorus of Emesa and Ammianus Marcellinus (Chang'ach, 2015). These claims were supported by a study conducted by James Harris and Edward Wente, who discovered that "the royal mummies of

2. Wall painting in the tomb of Sarenput II

Sarenput II was an ancient Egyptian nomarch (Great Chief or governor) who ruled some Egyptian provinces, including Elephantine, a small Nile island, during the reigns of pharaohs Senusret II and Senusret III of the 12th Dynasty. In 2017, his brother Shemai's tomb was excavated by a team of archaeologists, including Dr Alejandro Jimenez-Serrano. Dr. Alejandro was surprised when the team told him after a CT-scan that Shemia was a black African, most likely from neighbouring Nubia. (https://youtu.be/XAD_4lBCjR8). However, Live Science's report, published March 27, 2017, did not include this revelation. (https://www.livescience.com/58424-mummy-ancient-egyptian-nobleman-found.html).

3. The Great Sphinx, with the pyramid of Khafre

In 1787, during Count Constantine De Volney's visit, he observed the Sphinx head and said, "Just think, that this race of black men, today our slaves and the object of our scorn, is the very race to which we owe our arts, sciences, and even the use of speech."

4. Gold five guinea coins

Gold five guinea coins from West Africa were produced in England during the reigns of Charles II (1668-1684) and James II (1686-1688). The guinea coins were a tangible link between the City of London and the transatlantic slave trade.

CHAPTER 1

the 18th Dynasty, including the mummified remains of Amenhotep I, bore strong similarities to contemporary Nubians with slight differences" (Harris and Wente 1980). DNA Tribes Digest (2012) found that the DNA profiles of several 18th Dynasty mummies, including Tutankhamun and Amenhotep III, largely matched those of African populations south of the Sahara and, to a lesser extent, neighbouring populations.

In truth, the original or earliest inhabitants of ancient Egypt were represented by a variety of skin tones, just as they are today in Africa, and their cultural practices (i.e. artistic creativity, spiritual and ritual practices, divine kingship, the use of headrests, circumcision, matriarchal system, linguistics and hairstyles like the side lock and afro) are strikingly similar to those of modern African cultures, particularly those found among East African people. In addition, several ethnic groups south of the Sahara, including the Akan, Bamileke, Dogon, Ewe, Fula/Fulani, Kuba/Bakuba, Luo, Nguni, Igala, Igbo, Soninke, Tutsi/Watutsi, Wolof and Yoruba, claim to have migrated from ancient Egypt or the surrounding Nile Valley region. For example, the Igala people of Nigeria claim to have originated from ancient Egypt citing numerous similarities in vocabulary, cultures and burial practices. In fact, they claim to have fled ancient Egypt in the 8th century BCE due to famine, bad weather, wars and frequent foreign invasions (Adojoh, 2020). Furthermore, it is undeniable that the Kemetians or ancient Egyptians introduced the world to architecture, art, astronomy, writing, mathematics, as well as the techniques of surgery and embalming methods for the deceased. They had a significant impact on the modern world by laying the groundwork for the Greek and Roman civilisations, which in turn influenced today's Western-European cultures.

Prior to the discovery of gold in the Americas or elsewhere, gold mined and produced by the medieval West African empires of Ghana, Mali and Songhay was used to power the global economy. In fact, from 1000 to 1500 CE, West African gold was exported via the trans-Saharan trade routes and played an important role in sustaining Europe's economies. Research also revealed that some ancient African societies, such as the Egyptians, Dogons (Mali) and Shonas (Zimbabwe) had advanced knowledge of astronomy, while others across the continent were already smelting iron for agricultural, hunting and warfare tools. Iron smelting and toolmaking contributed significantly to the rise of several African kingdoms. One notable example was the Benin kingdom (southern Nigeria and not the present-day country of Benin), which rose to prominence around 900 CE and remained one of the major powers in pre-colonial West Africa up until the late 19th century. According to the Guinness Book of Records (1974 edition), the Edo people of Benin, built the longest earthworks walls in the world. The walls are thought to have taken 600 years to construct, making them four times the length of the Great Wall of China.

Unfortunately, little remains of the Benin Walls today because the British destroyed them in 1897 CE along with the king's palace and the entire Benin City. Following this unjustified destruction of hundreds of years of Benin history, British soldiers looted thousands of Benin cultural artefacts, many of which date back to the 16th century and included the well-known bronze plaques, metal works and ivory carvings. Many of these stolen treasures can be found in private collections and museums across the western world, including the British Museum (London), which houses the vast majority of the loot, the Ethnological Museum of Berlin (Germany), the Metro-

CHAPTER 1

5. Benin Bronzes

Two of thousands of Benin bronzes looted by the British from the ancient Benin Kingdom in 1897. These historical objects are now on display in museums throughout Europe and the United States.

politan Museum of Art (New York) and many more. This intended destruction and theft was not limited to the Benin kingdom; it also targeted other prosperous African city-states and kingdoms. To put it mildly, the level of violence used to subdue and deprive Africa of its essence appears to have been a deliberate strategy implemented by European nations in order to erase any evidence of Africa's former glory. This is most likely why there are so few historical buildings or monuments in Africa, especially south of the Sahara. In the last decade, some museums and collectors have begun to return small quantities of artefacts to their countries of origin, while others "are still caught in a colonial mindset", according to Juergen Zimmerer, a professor of global history at the University of Hamburg (Brown,

2018). Nonetheless, returning these artefacts does not lessen the gravity of the harm done to Africa, and full restitution is the only logical way to right the wrongs of the past.

COLONISATION AND ITS AFTERMATH

According to the United Nations, Africa is home to 54 independent countries (one-quarter of the world's total) and has over 2000 indigenous languages. This contradicts the false narrative that portrays Africa as one large country, ignoring cultural and political differences among its separate states. Majority of these countries' borders were artificially drawn by European colonial powers. The infamous Berlin Conference (aka Scramble for Africa), held in Germany from November 15, 1884 to February 26, 1885, brought rival European imperialist powers together to decide how Africa would be divided, with no regard for the indigenous people or their cultures. The invasion was led by France, Germany, Belgium, Spain, Portugal, Italy and the United Kingdom. By the beginning of the 1900s, they had partitioned Africa, with the exception of Liberia and Ethiopia into colonies and spheres of influence, imposing impractical states that were detached from ethnic realities. Essentially, they restructured African societies to meet European interests and goals. Additionally, they aggressively "exploited Africa's people, mineral resources, harbours, rivers and forests, and transferred all the wealth to build up the economic and political strength of their own countries" (Nkrumah, 2007), making no significant investments in local communities. This could explain why Africa is where it is today. There is little doubt that Europeans committed some of the most horrific atrocities in Africa, such as the genocide of more than 15 million Congolese under Belgian King

CHAPTER 1

Leopold II's supervision and the German extermination of tens of thousands of Herero and Nama people in German South-West Africa (present-day Namibia) between 1904 and 1907. Unfortunately, the legacy of colonisation is still affecting Africa today under the guise of neo-colonialism.

Despite the widespread belief that Africa is a poor continent, it is actually a resource-rich land with abundant minerals and natural resources, including coal, cobalt, lithium, manganese, diamonds, gold, silver, Tantalum, platinum, coltan, uranium, copper, iron rare earth metals, bauxite, petroleum (crude oil) and natural gas. In a 2017 Honest Accounts report funded by Global Justice Now, it was stated that "the African continent is rich, but the rest of the world profits from its wealth through unjust debt payments, multinational company profits and hiding proceeds from tax avoidance and corruption." Regardless of centuries of subjugation and exploitation, the African continent still holds enormous wealth, including 30% of the world's mineral reserves, 40% of its gold, 80% of coltan, which is required for modern technology and 60% of its uncultivated arable land. This demonstrates that Africa is not impoverished, as many Western media outlets portray, but rather exploited and poorly managed. Some of the factors that have contributed to Africa's underdevelopment include civil wars, political instability, poor governance, corruption, failing to receive a fair price for its natural resources on the international market and dealing with unfair borrowing rates/terms from western lenders, such as the International Monetary Fund (IMF) and the World Bank. To drive growth across Africa, a vast majority of its 54 member states signed the Africa Continental Free Trade Agreement (AfCFTA), which took effect in 2021 and aims to promote industrial development, increase economic integration, value addition and

6. African colonies after the Berlin conference of 1884-5

create a single continental market for goods and services in Africa. Given that Africa has the world's youngest population, with 70% under the age of 30, there is hope that it will become a major player in the global stage sooner rather than later.

Regrettably, Europe's economic relationship with Africa has not changed significantly since the 15th century, and many African countries remain trapped in the economic model left behind by their colonisers. Unfortunately, they have continued to extract and export resources with minimal or no added value. Western nations and institutions support the strategy of keeping African countries at the raw material end of the value chain (Benyera, 2021). This shows that Western powers have little interest in Africa's development. However, in recent years, some African countries, including DR Congo, Ghana, Namibia and Zimbabwe, have taken the bold step of enacting policies that ban or restrict the export of critical materials in their raw state. This realignment of their export strategies as specified under AfCFTA will ensure that raw materials are processed locally, encouraging industrialisation in their respective economies. Some observers believe that their strategy "faces bottlenecks...such as poor energy [supply], inadequate road [and rail] infrastructure, difficult political environments and a lack of adequate technical, financial, and human capital" (Schulz, 2020). It is expected that once these issues have been effectively addressed and capacity has been built to process these minerals locally, both foreign and domestic investors will commit resources to processing in various African countries. Moreover, most African countries will see growth in wealth, employment and a reduction in poverty. They will also have enough resources to sustain their growing populations. In fact, the signs are very promising as indicated by the president of the African Development Bank Group, who stated at a summit in May 2024 that "11 out of the 20 fastest growing economies in the world in 2023 were African" (Ben Yedder, 2024).

Chapter 2

A TO Z CHARACTERS FROM AFRICA

ALKEBULAN

There is a school of thought that claims that Africa's most ancient indigenous name was Alkebulan. When you search for the name *Alkebulan* on the internet, the results do not provide a credible source for its origin. However, the existence of the name is usually attributed to the late Dr Cheikh Anta Diop, the famous Senegalese historian. In fact, Diop never mentioned that name in any of his published works. A more thorough search of the internet revealed that the earliest source of the name Alkebulan was Andre Thevet's 1575 book *Cosmographie Universelle* (Universal Cosmography). In the legend to his map of Africa, he wrote "Having described the kingdoms, provinces, mountains, rivers, gulfs and promontories of this part of the world which we call AFRICA, the Greeks [called] Lybia and the Arabs [called] Alkebulan ..." (Thevet, 1575).

The late Black scholar Dr. Yosef Ben Jochanan made the next mention of Alkebulan in his 1972 book called *Black Man of the Nile and his Family*, claiming that it meant *Mother of Mankind* or *Garden of Eden*.

He also stated that among the many names of Alkebulan were the following: Ethiopia, Corphye, Ortegia, Libya and Africa, the latest of all. Dr Ben attested that Alkebulan was the oldest and only one of indigenous origin. He claimed that it was used by the Moors, Nubians, Numidians, Khart-Haddans [Carthagenians] and Ethiopians. Lastly, he linked the name Africa to the ancient Greeks and Romans. Unfortunately, Dr Ben did not provide a source for where he obtained the information. However, he was an advocate of Alkebulan and opposed the name Africa. In the 1980's, Dr. Ben became well-known for leading guided tours to Kemet (Egypt) and the Nile Valley Civilisations (Nubia, Sudan and Ethiopia).

Over the centuries, various names have been given to different parts of the African continent. Historians have long disagreed about the origin of one of those names, *Africa*. Most believe it came from words used by ancient Phoenicians, Greeks and Romans. The two most likely words that inspired the Romans to name their colonial province in Northern Africa (present-day Tunisia and eastern Algeria) are the Latin word *aprica*, which means sunny, and the Greek word *aphrike*, which means without cold. By the end of the late 17th century, the name Africa had been applied on the entire continent. Some Africans both on the continent and in the diaspora question whether the name Africa is still appropriate because it was given by European colonisers and they have called for a change. They are leaning toward Alkebulan, but there is no conclusive evidence that the name is indigenous.

CHAPTER 2

BAOBAB

The Baobab (pronounced *bau-bab* or *bay-oh-bab*) tree is one of Africa's oldest life forms which can withstand high temperatures and long periods of drought. Out of the 8 species of baobab in existence, six are native to Madagascar, one native to Australia and the last species is native to mainland Africa. The mainland African species, *Adansonia digitate* (aka African Baobab) have been known to live for more than 3,000 years, reach heights of 30 meters (about 98 feet) and have a circumference or trunk diameter of more than 10 metres (32.8 feet). Its hollow trunk is fire-resistant and can hold a large amount of water. This icon of the African landscape is often described as the *upside-down* tree because when leafless, the bare branches resemble roots sticking up into the air. In addition, these massive and distinctive trees are deeply intertwined with local cultures and traditions, and they are cited in countless African mythologies and folklore. The baobab tree grows in 32 African countries, mostly in the savannah regions south of the Sahara. This remarkable tree was introduced in ancient times to south Asia and can now be found on several Caribbean islands, including Barbados, Antigua, Jamaica and St. Croix in the US Virgin Islands, where enslaved Africans brought the seeds with them on their trans-Atlantic voyage.

For centuries, several African societies have relied on the Baobab tree for its nutritional values and medicinal qualities. Its inherent health benefits were overlooked by European explorers, who made no mention of them during their colonisation of Africa. The communities where this incredible tree grows have long referred to it as the *Tree of Life*, because every part of it is useful in the most important aspects of everyday life. For example, the whitish fruit pulp of the baobab, often known as *monkey bread*, is extremely nutritious and has a very high vitamin C content (Bamalli, et al., 2014), as well as containing B vitamins, calcium, potassium, phosphorus, magnesium and iron. Furthermore, the seeds, leaves, roots, tubers, twigs and flowers are all edible and commonly used in traditional medicine, while the inner bark fibre is used to make baskets, rope, clothing and a variety of other products. The mighty Baobab tree also provides food and shelter to a wide range of mammal and bird species, from the smallest insect to the mighty African elephant. In many African societies, the Baobab tree symbolises strength, resilience and its connection between the supernatural and the physical world.

Although Western or European society became aware of the Baobab tree in the mid-18th century, it took decades for them to understand and promote its health benefits, which Africans had known for centuries. The baobab fruit has even been dubbed the ultimate *superfruit* due to its nutritional values and its ability to prevent a variety of diseases. Many Western companies are now producing natural organic baobab powder as a food supplement to boost the immune system's resistance to disease and infection. Following a 12-year study (2005-2017) of over 60 very large African Baobab trees, the scientific journal *Nature Plants* reported in June 2018 that 8 of the 13 oldest trees and 5 of the 6 largest trees had collapsed or died across Southern Africa (Patrut, 2018). Some experts believe it is the result of man-made climate change, but more research is needed to prove this conclusively. Despite this, the iconic Baobab tree is thriving on the African continent.

CHAPTER 2

COWRIE SHELLS

Cowrie (also spelt cowry) is the shell of a small snail-like creature that lives in the warm and shallow waters of the Indian and Pacific Oceans' shores and lagoons. It is estimated that there are over 200 species. Cowrie shells, specifically *Monetaria Moneta* (aka money cowrie), were long used as currency in almost every part of the world, making them the first global currency. Until the early 20th century CE, two Indo-Pacific species, *Monetaria Moneta* and *Monetaria Annulus* (formerly *Cypraea Moneta* and *Cypraea Annulus*), served as currency for the exchange of goods and services in Africa. The former was more widely used in West Africa and originated on the coast of the Maldives in the Indian Ocean. The latter were primarily sourced from the East African coast, where they are abundant and occur naturally. Furthermore, the first documented widespread use of cowrie shells as a medium of exchange in West Africa took place in the Mali Empire (1238-1488), one of the region's greatest empires in the 14th century CE. However, Arab travellers such as al-Bakri and Ibn Battuta, reported in the 11th and 14th centuries that cowrie shells of the *M.moneta* species were used in various ways in parts of West Africa, as early as the 10th century CE (Hopkins and Levtzion, 2000, as cited in Haour, 2016).

The earliest historical evidence about the use of cowries in West Africa, shows that they were transported via the trans-Saharan trade routes. This changed when the Europeans arrived and began shipping goods across the Atlantic Ocean. According to historical records, the Portuguese were the first Europeans to import *M.moneta* cowries into West Africa in 1515 (Odunbaku, 2012). The majority of demands for these cowries came from trade, which increased dramatically during the trans-Atlantic slave trade in the 16th century CE. Indeed, it is estimated that up to one-third of the enslaved Africans brought to the Americas to work on plantations were bought with this shell money (Yang, 2019). As the demand for cowries reached near-industrial levels in the 18th century CE, European merchants began to look for alternative sources of supply outside of the Maldives. They started importing large quantities of *M.annulus* cowries from East African countries like Mozambique and Zanzibar into West Africa, causing local currencies and economies to collapse. In the early 20th century, European powers established colonial monetary systems in their colonies, including currency boards. As a result, cowrie shells and other local currencies, such as gold dust, copper rings and salt were eliminated. They strengthened the colonial currency's dominance by mandating that local taxes, wages and other colonial transactions be paid in it. This resulted in European dominance around the world.

The actions of European colonial powers "ushered in a new economic regime that would eventually replace the local monetary order" (Fuller H, 2009). Consequently, Africans were denied the opportunity to establish and manage their own monetary system. Cowrie shells were much more valuable in West Africa than elsewhere on the African continent, which may explain why Ghana's cedi (currency) is named after them. Cowries were not only used as currency in Africa, but they were also regarded as a symbol of wealth, power and security. As a result, many women wore a good-luck charm necklace with one cowry around their waist or neck. Furthermore, cowrie shells, specifically M.annulus (aka Owo Ero in Yoruba), were used in rituals and divination in many African societies, particularly among the Yoruba people of southwest Nigeria (Odunbaku, 2012). Despite the fact that cowrie shells are no longer used as currency, they are still popular as decorations for jewellery, musical instruments, ritual sculptures such as masks, and to adorn clothing, plaited hair and headgear. Africans demonstrated their creativeness by using cowries in a variety of ways.

DRUM

African drums are a popular musical instrument that produces beautiful rhythms. They have been used since the beginning of time to commemorate humanity's relationship with the creator. Most of the drums are typically carved from solid logs of wood, with a drumhead or membrane made of dried and shaved animal skin, such as goat, deer, sheep or cow. In addition to wooden drums, Africans made drums out of metal, gourds [calabash] and earthenware [clay]. Some drums doubled as works of art, with images or decorations that had deep spiritual meaning or simply told a story. African drums come in a variety of heights, sizes and shapes, including tubular, hourglass, kettle, barrel and round. In ancient times, drums were used to communicate between ethnic groups that were thousands of miles apart. Most African communities used them to celebrate all aspects of life, such as announcing meetings, wars, or dangers, telling stories, and supporting traditional religious activities, traditional festivals and ceremonial functions like coronations, naming ceremonies, marriages and funerals.

African drums can be played with sticks, hands, or a combination of both. The Djembe (pronounced jem-beh and translated as those who gather together in peace) is the most well-known of these drums and it is available worldwide. The exact origins of this ancient drum are unknown, but historians generally agree that it was invented around the 12th century by the Bambara or Mandinka people of present-day

Mali, West Africa. However, the djembe gained popularity during the reign of the great Mali Empire (present-day Mali, Senegal, Gambia and Guinea). The empire flourished from 1235 to 1645 and was founded by the legendary warrior king Sundiata Keita (aka the Lion King), great-uncle of the 14th Century West African ruler, Mansa Musa, who is regarded as the richest person in history, with an estimated personal wealth equivalent of $400 billion. Today, the djembe remains an integral part of daily life in many West African societies.

A traditional Djembe drum, like many other African drums such as Atsimevu (Ghana and Togo), Gangan, Talking drum (Nigeria), Bata (Nigeria), Kaganu (Ghana and Togo), Ngoma (Eastern and Southern Africa), Kpanlogo (Ghana), Negarit, Lukumbi (DRC) and Bougarabou (Guinea, Gambia and Senegal), is carved from a single piece of African hardwood and has the power to ignite passion and creativity, express deep emotions and maintain overall health (mental, physical and spiritual). This could explain why African drums were banned in many parts of the Americas and the Caribbean during the days of slavery. European slavers feared the practice of African drumming, which they described as *hellish* and associated it with slave resistance. Drumming was so frowned upon that slave-owners who allowed their slaves to drum were fined heavily. However, the beating of drums by enslaved Africans represented freedom, while also sharing and preserving their African heritage. Furthermore, African drums have a deeper, symbolic and cultural significance because they are used in religious ceremonies and ritual practices to invoke the spirits of ancestors and deities, as well as to promote unity within the community. Most Africans consider the drum to be the heartbeat and soul of their communities, and it has long been used to promote African traditions, cultures and festivities.

ELEPHANT

African Elephants are the world's largest land animal and are easily recognised by their long trunks, which is used for smelling, breathing, drinking, trumpeting and picking up things. African elephants are classified into two subspecies: Savanna or Bush elephant (Loxodonta africana) and the Forest elephant (Loxodonta cyclotis). Although both species have grey skin, the forest elephant is smaller in size, accounts for one-quarter to one-third of the total African elephant population (World Wildlife Fund, n.d.) and can be found in Central and West Africa rainforests. These magnificent creatures have a strong social bond and live in family groups led by a female (the cow). Both African elephant species are known to use their large ears to regulate body temperature, while their tusks serve as a digger or a defense mechanism when fighting.

The African elephant, like its Asian cousin (Elephas maximus), is a highly intelligent animal with memories that span many years. In many traditional African societies, elephants represent wisdom, resilience, strength and longevity. The Maasai, Baka, Himba, Yoruba and Bambara are among the ethnic groups that value elephants in their cultures. They believe that these majestic creatures teach humans about the value of family, the strength of unity and the power of collective memory. Unfortunately, poaching and hunting activities pose a threat to these iconic symbols of Africa. Moreover, the growing human population is causing them to lose their traditional migratory routes and habitat. Between 2007 and 2014, the first continent-wide survey of Savannah elephants in Southern and Eastern Africa revealed a 30% decrease in population. The same downward trend was observed for Forest elephants, whose number fell by more than 60% between 2002 and 2011 (Lindsaya, 2017). If the unsustainable slaughter of African elephants continues, conservationists predict that they will become extinct within a few decades. To prevent this potential tragedy, elephant sanctuaries were established to ensure their safety. These sanctuaries can be found in countries, including Botswana, Angola, Namibia, Zimbabwe, Kenya, Tanzania and South Africa, with the former housing the continent's largest elephant population (approximately 130,000).

Protecting these massive mammals from poachers is critical, but should not to be the only consideration; trophy hunting of African elephants (a colonial-era practise) should also be explicitly banned. Supporters of trophy hunting believe that these expensive hunting trips will raise much-needed funds to preserve and restore wild population, as well as protect against poaching. Conservationists, on the other hand, argue that hunting endangered species is unethical and that killing elephants to save elephants does not make a compelling case. In the summer of 2022, a number of conservation and animal protection organisations from all over the world, including many African NGOs, condemned trophy hunting. One participant, Dr Mark Jones, Head of Policy at Born Free Foundation stated that "At Born Free, we have long campaigned for an end to trophy hunting on moral and ethical grounds…it cannot be right for European hunters to be able to pay to kill threatened wild animals…trophy hunting causes immense animal suffering while doing little or nothing for wildlife conservation or local communities…in many cases trophy hunters remove key individual animals from fragile populations, damaging their social and genetic integrity. It's time to bring trophy hunting to a permanent end…" ("Call for a ban on hunting," 2022).

CHAPTER 2

FAMILY

The family is extremely important in African societies, with the vast majority of people belonging to an extended family system. A traditional African family is made up of a man, his wife and their children, as well as aunties, uncles, grandparents, nieces, nephews, cousins, in-laws and other non-biologically family members. The child is central to this traditional institution, which can be patrilineal (descent through father), matrilineal (descent through mother), or a combination of the two. Furthermore, various adult members constantly influence and shape the child's character and personality. Some of these adults' primary responsibilities include teaching children the difference between right and wrong, cultivating a culture of respect and instilling a sense of community. In other words, children are raised together and given the necessary tools they need to become productive members of society. The African proverb, *It takes a village to raise a child* expresses this family perspective.

The extended family system is a strong social and economic unit that provides care, support, moral guidance and a variety of services. It offers protection and promotes the concept of *my brother's keeper* by caring for the poor, elderly, widowed and orphaned, which is one of the most cherished values in traditional African socio-economic arrangements (Mafumbate, 2019). However, factors such as the influx of foreign religions and cultures, education, urbanisation, technological advancements, migration and westernisation (European-driven ideologies, values and practices) continue to put pressure on the extended family's role as an effective nurturing and supporting system. According to some researchers, the extended family is deteriorating even more as a result of the sweeping wave of globalisation (an offshoot of colonialism) being driven by Western institutions such as CNN and BBC, social media sites, including Facebook and YouTube, the World Bank, World Trade Organisation (WTO), NGOs like Oxfam and Save The Children, and many United Nations agencies. Their influence, demands and programmes are leading to major changes in traditional African structures, such as marriage patterns, family sizes, gender roles, divorce rates, intergenerational relationships and kinship network dynamics (Adaki, 2023). Essentially, these will fundamentally alter how African families are represented and organised. Some analysts believe that modernisation which is based on globalisation, will help Africa to adapt to these changes, whereas others argue that in order for Africa to succeed in the future, it must look inward rather than outward and preserve its diverse and rich cultural heritage.

Despite the overwhelming influence of Western ideas, certain aspects of the traditional African family, such as traditional marriage practices and assistance to less fortunate extended family members, remain important in most African societies. This emphasises the idea that these societies have been socialised over many generations to believe in a culture of communalism rather than individualism. Aside from their resilience, these societies are constantly pressured to abandon their traditional family system in favour of the nuclear family system (parents and their children), which is common in many Western societies. This implies that Africans are being coerced into adopting the Western model, which will most likely weaken their own structures. Therefore, for Africa to develop and survive, its people must weigh the advantages and disadvantages of both systems before deciding which best reflects their cultural and social values. For example, most African communities consider childbearing as a means of ensuring the survival and continuity of their societies. As a result, choosing the wrong option can have severe long-term consequences. Reduced birth rates and smaller families are two of the effects that are already evident in many Western countries. This is a growing trend that is likely to result in labour shortages, higher debt and slower economic growth.

GOLD

Gold is one of many precious metals found throughout Africa. In ancient Egypt, "gold mining started in pre-dynastic times…ranging from open pits to moderate underground works." (Teeter, 2011). This precious metal was sometimes referred to as *the flesh of the gods*. Gold production was also a major activity in West Africa's first great empire, ancient Ghana (present-day Mauritania and Mali), or Wagadu (300-1276 CE), as its rulers called it. The Ghana Empire's history depicts a time when imperial power, trade and cultural exchange flourished in West Africa. Arab travellers and scholars wrote extensively about the Ghana Empire's vast gold reserves and production, referring to the powerful empire founded by the indigenous Soninke people as the *Land of Gold* and describing the presence of gold deposits in all of its regions. This ancient empire's rulers were given the title Ghana (warrior or war chief) and the king was also known as Kaya Maghan, which means *Lord of the Gold*. For over a thousand years, the West African empires of Ghana, Mali and Songhay were the world's major gold suppliers, accounting for two-thirds of the global gold supply.

Gold trading in West Africa dates back centuries, as documented by numerous travellers and historians. However, news of the enormous gold displayed by Mansa Musa, emperor of Mali from 1312-1337

CE, during his pilgrimage to Mecca (Islam's holiest city), caught the interest of Europeans, prompting them to start looking for gold in West Africa. As a result, trade between the Mali Empire and Europe expanded. For example, the Mali Empire was featured on a *Map of the World* in 1339 and Mansa Musa was shown holding a gold nugget on a 1375 Catalan Atlas. On the map, he was described as the richest and noblest king in the world.

This exposure to African gold was the inspiration needed by early European explorers to visit West Africa. In the 1400s and 1500s West Africa was the undisputed gold supplier to the rest of the world. The Portuguese were the first Europeans to explore West Africa (aka Guinea coast) for gold and other resources. Within a decade of arriving on the Gold coast (present-day Ghana) in 1471, they had built a fort in the gold producing region of Anomansa (traditional name of Elmina) and were already actively mining gold. By the second half of the 17th century, other European nations, including the Danes, Dutch, Swedes, French, English and traders from north German ports, quickly followed and established trading posts at various points in West Africa. In 1663, the Royal African Company shipped gold mined by Akan miners to London, where it was minted into coins for circulation in England (Adam, 2022).

African gold was extracted from a variety of sources, not limited to West African gold mines. East African city-states such as Mogadishu (Somalia), Mombasa (Kenya), Kilwa (Tanzania) and Sofala (Mozambique) obtained gold and other commodities from southern African interior settlements like Great Zimbabwe and exported them to Arabia, Persia, India and China (Rodland, 2021). Along with the extensive trade on the East African coast, native Africans, settled Muslim Arabs and Persian traders developed Swahili (swah-hee-lee), a language derived from Arabic and Bantu. The arrival of the Portuguese to acquire gold and other resources in 1498, resulted in the destruction of several Swahili states (Rodland 2021; Rothman 2002).

Africa remains one of the world's top gold-producing regions. Prior to 2007, South Africa was the world's largest gold producer, with the Witwatersrand basin accounting for about 40% of total global gold production. It is the richest gold field ever discovered. Not surprisingly, gold production in Africa has increased significantly in comparison to the rest of the world, with at least 10 African countries doubling their output. This has resulted in increased GDP in those countries. However, due to Africa's unregulated environment, much of this gold is stored in bank vaults in major cities around the world, with large amounts being smuggled out of the continent. This explains why Africa's largest gold exporters are not always the largest gold producers.

HERBALIST

Herbalists are traditional African healers, doctors, diviners, psychologists and consultants who practice a holistic approach to healing and treatment. They are well-known for using their extensive skills, vast knowledge of indigenous plants, incantations, divination and other methods to treat a variety of ailments, illnesses, misfortunes and bone injuries. These *native doctors*, whose practices and expertise are based on the customs and beliefs of their ancestors, as well as having an understanding of the visible and invisible world, are known by various indigenous names throughout Africa, including Babalawo by the Yorubas, Dibia by the Igbos and Sangoma or Nyanga by South Africans. According to Green (2009) as cited in Shizha and Charema

(2011), "Herbalists are so popular in Africa that any herb trading market in Durban is said to attract between 700,000 and 900,000 traders a year from South Africa, Zimbabwe and Mozambique." There are numerous herb markets all across the African continent. For herbalists, knowledge is passed down orally and their world-view sees humanity as inextricably linked to nature and everything in the universe, whereas the Western or European world-view sees nature as a collection of resources to be exploited to meet human needs (Maweu, 2011).

Traditional African Medicine (TAM) and healing practices were once seen by Eurocentric scholars as primitive, unscientific and backward. On the contrary, indigenous Africans are thought to have developed the world's oldest and most widely used healthcare system. In fact, the majority of the advancements made by western science and technology have their roots in indigenous knowledge (Maweu, 2011). Furthermore, before the arrival of European missionary doctors, Africans had already made significant medical advances. In the East African kingdom of Bunyoro (Western Uganda), for example, a Traditional Health Practitioner performed a caesarean section in 1879, much to the surprise of Dr. Robert W. Felkin, a Scottish medical missionary and anthropologist who witnessed the entire procedure and later used his observations to write his thesis (Bennett, 2019). This was not an isolated incident, as there is plenty of evidence to support the efficacy of TAMs and medical procedures. While the hundreds of millions of Africans (Up to 80% of the population) who seek the services of herbalists are typically poor and come from rural areas, they can rely on herbalists because they are easily accessible, affordable and their practices have been historically and culturally validated.

CHAPTER 2

Historically, Western pharmaceutical companies have exploited several African plants for their medical, pharmacological and therapeutic properties. Many of these companies went on to patent the medicines they developed, without consulting or compensating the communities who discovered the plant species. Due to the high cost of Western medicine and treatments, some African countries have taken commendable steps to incorporate traditional medicine into their national health care systems. According to a TAM review article, "the ratio of traditional healers to the population in Africa is 1:500 compared to 1:40,000 medical doctors" (Mahomoodally, 2013). The World Health Organisation (WHO) acknowledges traditional medicine as one of the most reliable alternatives for achieving global health care coverage and it appears that "the treatments and remedies used in TAM have gained more appreciation from researchers in western science" (Antwi-Baffour, et al., 2014). For the past two decades, Africa has observed *African Traditional Medicine Day* on August 31 each year as part of a strategy to strengthen the role of traditional medicine in national health systems.

As traditional medicine gains acceptance as a viable alternative to Western medicine, data collection becomes increasingly important in addressing safety, efficacy and quality concerns. This will ensure a relatively stable future for traditional medicine while also exposing humanity to thousands of years of diverse and rich indigenous knowledge practices. However, in order to comply with WHO guidelines and protocols, such as creating national herbal pharmacopoeias to document effective medicinal plants, local or regional traditional medicine associations must ensure that their skills, knowledge and practices are not exploited by this or other organisations.

IVORY

The majority of ivory comes from elephant tusks and may have a hard or soft texture. Hard (or yellow) ivory is brittle and found in West Africa, whereas soft (or white) ivory is moister, easier to work with and found in East Africa. In the past, ivory was used to make jewellery and small sculptures in Africa. Interestingly, ivory objects were present in ancient Egypt during both the Predynastic and Early Dynastic periods. According to Krzyszkowska and Morkot (2000), the majority of Egyptian Ivory came from Upper Nubia, which is now northern and central Sudan. In 1903, archaeologists excavated an ancient Egyptian site and discovered two carved ivory pharaoh statuettes. One represented a First Dynasty ruler, while the other depicted Khufu, a Fourth Dynasty (Old Kingdom) pharaoh who built the Great Pyramid of Giza. However, the high demand for ivory dates back to Europe's colonisation of Africa, which resulted in the slaughter of thousands of African elephants. Commercial interests in Europe drove up demand for elephant tusks, which were used to make ivory products such as billiard balls, piano keys and cutlery handles.

The reward for selling ivory (aka white gold) was the driving force behind the illegal hunting of African elephants. The ivory-driven hunting was so intense in the 1970s and 1980s that the African elephant population fell dramatically from 1.3 million to 600,000. For example, from 1969 to 1989, the price of uncarved ivory in Kenya increased by 3,500% (Lemieux & Clarke, 2009). This was one of the several incidents that prompted member states of the Convention on International Trade in Endangered Species of Wild Fauna and Flora (CITES) to impose a global ban on the sale of ivory sales in 1989. The goal was to reverse the decline of the African elephant population.

Despite the ban and numerous efforts to prevent the trade of ivory, thousands of elephants are still hunted to maintain the ivory trade. The World Wide Fund for Nature (formerly the World Wildlife Fund) estimates that 20,000 African elephants are killed each year for their ivory. Others believe it is closer to 30,000. According to several sources, Asia, particularly China, accounts for the majority of ivory demand, fueling the illegal ivory trade in countries such as Kenya and Tanzania. Notwithstanding the Chinese government's claims that it is addressing this issue, it is widely acknowledged that if current trend continues, African elephants may become extinct within decades.

JOLLOF

The term *Jollof* refers to a popular West African rice dish. It is thought to have originated in the ancient Jolof Empire (aka Jollof, Wolof and Wollof), which flourished from 1350 CE to 1549 CE in what is now Senegal, The Gambia and Mauritania. Jolof was a Wolof state that formed an empire or confederacy, with three other Wolof-speaking states (Kajoor, Bawol and Waalo) and other Senegambian peoples. The spread of Jollof rice in Senegal and other parts of West Africa coincided with the rise and influence of the Jolof Empire. The ancient empire disintegrated after a battle in the mid-16th century and each state under its control became independent kingdoms. Jolof attempted to reconquer Kajoor several times in the late 16th and early 17th centuries, but none of its efforts were successful (Charles, 1977). Following the dissolution of its vassal states, Jolof was reduced to a kingdom before being conquered by the French in the 19th century.

Jollof rice was originally known as Benachin, which translates to *one pot* in Wolof. Its popularity extends across West Africa, including Senegal, Ghana, Nigeria, Gambia, Mali, Ivory Coast, Sierra Leone, Liberia and Cameroon. These countries are now competing over who makes the best Jollof, resulting in a *Jollof rice war*. The significance of this iconic rice dish can also be felt across the Americas, due to the trans-Atlantic slave trade, when millions of West African slaves stretching from Senegambia region to Liberia (aka Rice Coast) were traded and exploited for their labour. Many of these enslaved Africans brought with them agricultural methods and rice cultivation skills to the new world (in places like the Carolinas in the US, Surinam and Mexico) and they are thought to have influenced variations of rice dishes similar to Jollof rice in the US, Latin America and the Caribbean region. Jollof rice is made with rice, fresh tomatoes, onions, salt and chilli peppers. Fish, meat, vegetables and spices can all be added. Jollof rice can be prepared in a variety of ways, but the basic ingredients remain the same. Regardless of the authenticity debate among countries where Jollof rice is a national delicacy, history credits the Senegalese with inventing the rice dish.

KILIMANJARO

Mt. Kilimanjaro (nicknamed the *Roof of Africa*) is Africa's highest mountain and the world's fourth highest. It was formed about 3 million years ago and is located in Tanzania, near the Kenyan border. This *mountain of greatness* is the world's tallest free-standing mountain, rising at 19,341 feet (5,895 metres) above sea level and not part of a mountain range. Although the exact origin of the name Kilimanjaro is unknown, it is thought to be a combination of the Swahili word Kilima, which means mountain and the Chagga tribe (Tanzania) word Njaro, which loosely translates as whiteness or snow, resulting in the name *White Mountain*. Kilimanjaro and its surrounding forests were designated as Kilimanjaro National Park in 1973, and the United Nations Educational, Scientific and Cultural Organization (UNESCO) named the protected area as a World Heritage site in 1987, citing its unique environment.

Additionally, Kilimanjaro is an ancient dormant mountain with three volcanic cones: Shira (4,005 m), Mawenzi (5,140 m) and Kibo (5,895 m). The latter is the highest peak and is still considered active (rather than extinct). The highest point on Kibo's crater rim is called Uhuru, which is the Swahili word for *Freedom*. According to a National Geographic article, scientists believe the mountain last erupted 360,000 years ago. This giant of the African rift valley supports five major ecological zones: cultivated land, rain forest, moorland, alpine desert and an arctic summit. The weather in the mountains ranges from hot to bitterly cold. Since its first climb in 1889, Kilimanjaro has become a popular hiking destination for both locals and visitors. It is estimated that tens of thousands of people climb the mountain each year. Unfortunately, the remnants of the ice cap that once encircled Africa's king of mountains are rapidly disappearing due to large-scale atmospheric circulation changes (i.e. reduced snowfall and precipitation) and, to a lesser extent, global warming. Experts estimate that "the majority of the ice will be gone by 2040" (Africa Geographic, 2021; Mote & Kaser, 2007).

LION

Lions are the world's second largest member of the cat family, after tigers and the largest on the African continent. They are the only cats that live in large family groups, or prides. A typical pride can have 15 to 40 members, including one or two males, a dozen or so related females and their dependent offspring. As the cubs mature, young females will join their mother's pride and remain there for the rest of their lives, whereas young males will leave their birth pride to form their own. These social animals are carnivorous by nature and can live for 10-14 years in the wild. Male lions are 50% larger than females and have a distinctive thick mane of hair around their heads, which females do not have. According to experts, lions with darker manes are more dominant and will almost certainly win the fight to mate with females. They are also more intimidating to other males and will defend their pride's territory (West, 2005). Female lions, aka lionesses, are primarily responsible for hunting within their prides, whereas male lions hunt much larger preys such as buffalo. Lions typically hunt at night or early in the morning, as their eyes are well adapted to darkness.

Lions were once found all over the world, but they are now mostly found in Africa, south of the Sahara, particularly in Southern and Eastern Africa. Tanzania is home to the vast majority of African lions. These magnificent creatures are referred to as the *King of the Beasts* or *King of the Jungle*. Surprisingly, the Swahili word for lion is Simba, which also means king, strong and aggressive. Most African traditions associate the male lion with strength, courage and pride, while the lioness represents femininity, motherhood and the moon. Ancient Egyptian cultures recognised the qualities of the lion, as evidenced by the features of the Great Sphinx of Giza, which has a lion body and a human head resembling a pharaoh. Also, the Shona people of southern Africa have a strong affinity for lions. Their traditional society preserved and protected them. Lions are revered as mediums for Shona ancestors and protectors of their land. The sighting of a lion was interpreted as a sign of safety for the land and people (Taringa, n.d.). Therefore, killing a lion was an offense. Although the lion population in Africa is declining, it is not classified as endangered or threatened.

MADAGASCAR

Madagascar, formerly known as the Malagasy Republic, is an island nation in the Indian Ocean, off the coast of South East Africa. It is Africa's largest island, covering over 587,040 square kilometres (approximately 226,658 square miles) and the world's fourth largest after Greenland, New Guinea and Borneo. Archaeologists believe the island and India, separated from Africa, which was once part of the Gondwana supercontinent around, 160 million years ago. India and Madagascar eventually separated around 88 million years ago, leaving Madagascar isolated for millions of years. As a result, it produced a diverse range of rare plants, exotic birds and species of animals, including the lemur and giant Baobab (Adansonia grandidieri). Due to the island's isolation for millions of years, 90% of its wildlife is found nowhere else on the planet. Madagascar is also known as the home of the Baobab tree, which has six of the world's eight species. Its inhabitants, known as Malagasy people, can trace their ancestors to Southeast Asia, Africa, the Near East and India. The most widely spoken languages are French and Malagasy.

AMAZING AFRICA

7. Collage 1 (L-R)

The mighty Africa Baobab tree, Cowrie shells on mask, Catalan Atlas, ca. 1375, showing Mansa Musa holding a giant gold nugget, The majestic African lion

Madagascar, like the rest of Africa, has had strong kingdoms and empires in the past. Sakalava, Betsimisaraka and Merina were among the most influential. The latter emerged in the late 18th century and began military conquests in other regions. Following a treaty signed with the British in 1820, the Merina sovereign was recognised as King of Madagascar. It rose to power in the early 19th century, defeating all of its rivals with British weapons and military training (Campbell, 2016). However, owing to counter attacks from local adversaries and waning loyalty among Merina subjects as a result of excessive forced labour, the French were able to invade Madagascar in 1893 and successfully end the Merina Empire's reign after two years of fighting. By 1897, Madagascar had become a French colony, with the sole purpose of extracting timber and exotic spices like vanilla. It achieved independence from France in 1960. Madagascar is surrounded by numerous smaller islands, including the Comoros, Mauritius, Reunion and Mayotte. Mozambique is the nearest African mainland country. With a diverse population of just over 30 million people (2023), Madagascar is a melting pot of 18 recognised ethnic groups, most of which have their origin in Asia and Africa.

NILE

The Nile is widely regarded as the world's and Africa's longest river. It flows for about 4,160 miles (6,693 kilometres) across northeast Africa, with two major tributaries: the White Nile and the Blue Nile. The White Nile begins at a section of Lake Victoria in Uganda, Africa's largest lake and the world's largest tropical lake. Nonetheless, some believe that its most distant source is the Ruvyironza River in Burundi or the Nyabarongo River from Rwanda's Nyungwe Forest

(Pedersen, 2016). The Blue Nile's source is undisputed, as it flows from Lake Tana in Ethiopia and supplies the majority of the Nile's water. Both rivers meet near Khartoum, Sudan's capital and flow from south to north before emptying into the Mediterranean Sea. This makes the Nile one of the world's most important northward-flowing rivers. Aside from Egypt, the Nile flows through ten other African countries: Burundi, Tanzania, Rwanda, DRC, Kenya, Eritrea, Uganda, Sudan, Ethiopia and South Sudan. During the course of its travels, the Nile passes through a variety of ecosystems ranging from tropical rainforests to extensive swamplands, before arriving in the desert. Moreover, the Nile supports a large number of animal, plant and bird species.

For thousands of years, the Nile has been a vital source of life for communities that surround it. This massive river brought fresh water, food and transportation to ancient Egypt and the Nubian Kingdom of Kush (now Sudan). It also provided them with fertile farmland. The ancient Egyptians named the river Ar or Aur (black) after the rich and fertile black sediment left behind by the river's annual flooding, which occurs between June and September. The flooding of the Nile was only brought under control after the Aswan High Dam was completed in 1970. Furthermore, the majority of Egypt's historical sites, such as Luxor, Cairo and Aswan, are located along the Nile's banks. The river's accessibility was an important transportation route for ancient Egyptians, allowing them to trade both locally and internationally. In addition, there was a strong link between the ancient Egyptian civilisation and this magnificent river, which may have been why the Greek historian Herodotus, who explored Egypt in the 5th century BCE, referred to Egypt as the *gift of the Nile*, because "without the (floodwaters) of the river, (ancient) Egypt would not exist" (Mokhtar,

1990, p.11). Other major African rivers includes the Zambezi in the Southeast; the Congo in the Southwest; and the Niger, Benue and Senegal in the West.

OWARE

Oware is an ancient African board game from the Mancala family of games (pit and pebble). The exact origin is unknown, but it has been linked to ancient Sumeria (Asia) and ancient Egypt (Africa). Evidence suggests that the game was discovered among Egyptian ruins dating back to 1400 BCE, with Stone Mancala boards carved into temples in Memphis, Thebes and Luxor. The Akan people of Ghana named the game Oware, which is considered a game for royalty and plays an important role in society. According to Asante (also spelt Ashante) legend, "Oware was used in 1700s Ghana by Ashante King Katakyie Opoku Ware I to resolve issues between married couples" (Bayeck, 2018). Hence its name Oware or Wari, which means he/she marries in the Asante language of Twi. Oware is widely regarded as one of the most popular indigenous African board games, as well as the national game of present-day Ghana.

This strategic and popular board game has numerous variations that are played throughout West Africa, West Central Africa, the Caribbean and the East Coast of South America. Oware is also known as Ayo-Olopon in south-west Nigeria, Awale in Ivory Coast and Benin, Wari in Mali, Ouril in Cape Verde, Adji in Ewe, and Warri in Barbados and Antigua and Barbuda. The Bao is another popular variation of the Mancala family game played in East Africa, particularly in Swahili-speaking countries. It is a game that requires complex mental calculation, similar to Oware, but it is played on a 2x8 game board rather than the 2x6 game board used in Oware. The game of Oware is typically played by two people on a board with two straight rows of six holes (referred to as Houses) and 48 seeds or stones evenly distributed between them. Each player controls six houses on their side of the board and takes turns capturing the most seeds. The player with more than 24 seeds wins the game. However, oware can be played by one or up to six people.

Playing oware was a way for Africans forced to work on colonial slave plantations in the Caribbean and other parts of the Americas to bond, remember their African roots and connect with their ancestors. Even centuries after Oware's arrival in the Caribbean, "it is now played much less frequently than in the past" (Stoffle et al., 2016). Oware has been described as an effective educational tool for improving cognitive and motor skills. The game is said to teach patience and discipline, communication, numeracy, problem solving, decision making and negotiation skills. According to the Oware Society's website, the adult version of oware is known as Abapa and the children's version is called Nam-nam. Because the Abapa requires a high level of calculation, it is mostly played during tournaments and promotional events. Oware's popularity has led to the development of digital versions of the strategic game, as well as the establishment of annual international oware tournaments. The game is unique in that if players do not have access to the board or digital version, they can dig holes in the ground and play with small stones, beads, or seeds instead.

CHAPTER 2

PYRAMID

Egypt is home to the world's most recognisable and famous pyramids. The Giza Pyramids are one of Africa's well-known traditional architecture structures, built as a final resting place for Egypt's royalty. They were constructed on the Giza plateau by Pharaohs Khufu (2575-2566 BCE), Khafre (Khufu's son) and Menkaure (Khafre's son). Khafre built the Great Sphinx, which is now regarded as one of ancient Egypt's most visible symbols. The Great Pyramid of Khufu was the first, oldest and largest of the three pyramids, covering over 13 acres (equivalent to about 10 football fields). It was completed in 2560 BCE and was made up of approximately 2.5 million limestone blocks, each weighing an average of 2.5 to 15 tonnes. Khufu's pyramid is still regarded as the world's largest and most finely crafted stone monument. According to Egyptologists, the Great pyramid took about 20 years to build and was intended to serve as Khufu's final resting place. Interestingly, the Giza pyramids are said to be aligned with the three stars of Orion's belt. The magnificent Egyptian pyramids demonstrate the ancient Egyptian civilisation's ingenuity and power.

Pyramids were built not only in ancient Egypt, but throughout Africa. From the 11th century BCE to the 4th century CE, the ancient Kingdom of Kush in Nubia (now Sudan) built over 300 pyramids. Kush, with its abundance of gold and other precious metals, reached its peak of power in the 8th century BCE, when it conquered ancient Egypt and expanded its influence across the Mediterranean, the Middle East and all the way into central Africa. Kush's pyramids are smaller and steeper than those in neighbouring Egypt, but they are still impressive, richly decorated and designed as tombs and monuments. Pyramids or pyramid shaped structures have also been found in other parts of

Africa, including Ethiopia, Libya and Zimbabwe. The construction of these structures clearly shows the greatness of many ancient African civilisations. Despite the abundance of evidence of pyramids and other ancient structures scattered throughout Africa, some people continue to deny that Africans were capable of such architectural accomplishments. Much of this viewpoint is motivated by racism, but advances in research and understanding of the archaeological record are disproving these myths.

QUEEN

Throughout history, African women have occupied positions of influence and power. Some of these women were great queens of honour and included Hatshepsut (fifth pharaoh of the Eighteenth Dynasty) of Egypt, Candace Amanirenas of the Kingdom of Kush (Sudan), Kahina, Berber/Imazighen (Algeria & Tunisia), Kambasa of Bonny Kingdom (Nigeria), Ranavalona I (Madagascar), Nzinga of Angola, Amina of Zaria (Nigeria), Gudit or Yodit (Ethiopia), Nyarroh of Bandasuma (Sierra Leone), Ndeta Yalla of Waalo Kingdom (Senegal), Yargoje of Zamfara (Nigeria) and Abla Pokou - Queen and founder of the Baoule people (subgroup of the Ashante ethnic group located in the Ivory Coast). These queens were more than just a king's wife; they led armies into battles, carried out massive expansion programmes, promoted long-distance trade and diplomatic relations, resisted colonial invasions and ruled over kingdoms and empires as sole protectors and holders of absolute power.

Queen Nzinga, aka Ann Zingha (1582-1663) of Angola, for example, was a tenacious leader who transformed her kingdoms of Ndongo and Matamba (located in present-day Angola) into a formidable commercial state on par with Portuguese colonies. As a brilliant strategist, she fought tirelessly against Portuguese colonial rule in order to liberate her people from slavery. For example, she was known for organising raiding parties to free captives on slave ships and providing refuge to escaped slaves. She eventually led the resistance to European imperialism in Africa. Queen Nzinga was one of Africa's most powerful female rulers, skilled in politics, diplomacy and strategy. She is held up as a symbol of bravery and resistance.

Queen Amina of Zaria (1533-1610) was another influential female leader. She was said to have used her strategic military skills to increase the wealth of her kingdom Zazzau (aka Zaria Emirate, which is located in present-day Nigeria) and gained control of many important trade routes throughout northern Nigeria. Zazzau was among several Hausa city-states. Queen Amina is also said to have commanded an army of 20,000 well-trained soldiers and was responsible for building the famous Zaria protective earthen city walls fortifications, many of which can still be seen today. Among the Hausa, Queen Amina is revered as a legend and her legendary exploits earned her the title *Amina, daughter of Nikatau; a woman as capable as a man.*

The stories of these brave and heroic women's resilience and accomplishments, most of which came from Africa's rich oral traditions, have had a significant impact on the African continent. Additionally, these legendary women did not only inspire some of Africa's most well-known states, but they also exemplified the spirit and strength of womanhood. Their very existence and reign show that ancient Africa has long supported female leadership and authority, far longer than any other region of the world, including the well-documented Greek and Roman civilisations.

RHINOCEROS

The rhinoceros, or rhino, is the second-largest land mammal after elephants. Two of the five rhino species live in Africa, with the remaining three in Asia. African rhinos are classified into two species: black rhinos (Diceros bicornis) and white rhinos (Ceratotherium simum). These extremely strong and powerful animals are herbivores, which means they only consume plants. Both African species are dark grey-brown in colour, with two horns of varying sizes and a keen sense of smell. However, white rhinos are larger than black rhinos, weighing between 1,800 and 3,000 kg, while black rhinos weigh between 900 and 1,350 kg. Rhinos, despite their weight, can outrun any human on record. These iconic species were once found in the wild across Africa, south of the Sahara, but are now mainly found in a few countries within east and southern Africa; with "South Africa, the stronghold of the species...also a hub for poaching" (Lunstrum, 2014, as cited in Mamba, 2018).

The trade in rhino horn has a long history, with it being used for medicine, carving figurines, cups and plates and as an aphrodisiac. During Africa's colonial period (mainly in the 1800s), early European settlers killed thousands of these prehistoric mammals for their horns, causing their population to rapidly decline. Between 1849 and 1895, one data source reported that 11,000 kg of rhino horn was traded annually in East Africa. This equates to approximately 170,000 black rhinos killed during that time period (Leader-Williams, 1992, as cited in Martin and Martin 1982). The most alarming decline in Africa's rhino population, particularly the black rhino, occurred during the 1970s and 1980s, when both species faced extinction due to widespread poaching and habitat loss. At the time, North Yemen had the highest demand for rhino horns, which were used to make *prestigious* traditional curved dagger (jambiya) handles. According to Vigne and Martin, 2018, an estimated "8 tonnes of African rhino horn left the continent each year, representing a total of 30,000 mainly black rhinos killed in that decade for exports alone." In fact, "between 1970 and 1992, black rhino numbers suffered a 96% reduction in Africa" (Mamba, 2018). Other major rhino horn importers in the 1970s included China, Taiwan, Japan and South Korea.

In recent years, rhino poaching has escalated due to increased illegal consumer demand for horns, which was coming mainly from mainland China and Vietnam, where they are used in traditional medicine or carved into high-value artistic objects. Rhino horns have long been used as an essential ingredient in Chinese traditional medicine and they are widely believed to have medicinal properties that can aid in the treatment of hangovers, fever and terminal illnesses such as cancer. This is puzzling because rhino horn is entirely composed of keratin, a naturally produced protein found in human hair, nails and the outer layer of the skin. Nonetheless, experts agree that there is no *scientific* evidence to support the claim of the medicinal value of rhino horn. Although CITES currently prohibits international trade in rhino horn, African rhinos are still at risk of extinction. To ensure the survival of both African rhino species, additional measures to combat the illegal rhino horn trade will be necessary. This will necessitate collaboration among international agencies as well as genuine commitment from governments at all levels.

SAHARA

The Sahara Desert (aka Sahra in Arabic, which means desert) is the world's largest hot desert, stretching from the Atlantic Ocean in the west to the Red Sea in the east. It runs through ten African countries, including Algeria, Chad, Egypt, Libya, Mali, Mauritania, Morocco, Niger, Sudan and Tunisia. This famous desert is nearly the size of China or the United States, covering an area of 9,200,000 square kilometres (3,600,000 square miles). The Sahara is made up of 30% sand dunes and sheets, with the remaining 70% consisting mostly of rocky plains covered in stones and gravel. Other landscape features of the Sahara include salt flats, mountains, dry valleys, streams and oasis. The Sahara is not always scorching hot as many have been led to believe; however, it receives very little rainfall, resulting in hot days and cool nights.

The Sahara desert was once abundant with lakes, forests, trees, plants, wildlife and animals. The region's ancient cave paintings, which date from 8000 or 7000 BCE, depict images of people and animals such as hippopotamus, elephants and giraffes. According to an MIT news online article, the Sahara's *green* era lasted from 11,000 (9,000 BCE) to 5,000 (3,000 BCE) years ago and is thought to have ended in less than two centuries (Chu, 2013). The article also mentioned an MIT study, which discovered that the Sahara and North Africa as a whole alternate between wet and dry climates every 20,000 years. With an average annual rainfall of 3 inches (7.6 centimetres), the Sahara desert is one of the world's driest regions. Because of the dryness of the environment, large orange dust storms are transported by wind across the globe each year to the Mediterranean, parts of Europe, South America, Central America, the Caribbean and the southern

United States. Despite its harsh landscape, the Sahara is home to approximately 2.5 million people as well as a diverse range of plant and animal species including antelopes and gazelles. The various communities living in the Sahara have adapted to the region's extremely dry conditions.

The effects of desertification is visible in many parts of the world and the United Nations estimates that 30 million acres of land are lost annually. In Africa, the Sahel, a region south of the Sahara, is the most vulnerable to desertification. With a population of around 150 million people, this critical region stretches from Senegal on the Atlantic coast to Eritrea on the Red Sea coast. It is also prone to droughts, water scarcity (as rivers and lakes drying up) and the loss of fertile land. This prompted the countries bordering the Sahara to launch the *Great Green Wall* initiative. The goal is to prevent desertification in the region by planting millions of trees. According to a National Science Foundation study published in 2018, scientists discovered that the Sahara desert has expanded by around 10% over the last century, which they attribute to natural climate cycles that affect rainfall and in part, human-caused climate change. The study concluded that if climate change persists, the Sahara will continue to expand.

TIMBUKTU

Timbuktu (also spelt Timbuctoo) is an ancient city in Mali, West Africa. It was founded around 1100 CE by Nomadic Tuaregs from the Sahara and grew into a town, then a city with permanent settlements. Timbuktu was a significant commercial, religious and cultural centre, and its residents travelled to neighbouring African states to learn and engage in business activities (Shuriye and Ibrahim, 2013).

By the 14th century, Timbuktu had become part of the Mali Empire and flourished as a trans-Saharan gold and salt trading centre. It was incorporated into the expanding Songhai state in 1468 and remained so until 1591. Timbuktu, which was five times the size of medieval London, was also a major Islamic centre, with the prestigious Sankore University attracting scholars and thousands of students from all over the Muslim world. It was known for having the best educational standards in the world. The ancient manuscripts and priceless books found in this desert town show that oral history was not the only way Africans recorded their history. In 1973, a manuscript library and research institute were established in Timbuktu to preserve and store the region's extensive manuscript collections. Today, the library named after Ahmed Baba (1564-1627 CE), the famous 16th/17th century scholar, houses nearly 30,000 manuscripts. Many old West African families also own thousands of manuscripts dating back hundreds of years.

Moroccan invaders conquered and seized Timbuktu in 1591, using superior firearms. Two years later, on October 15, 1593, scholars, their families and associates were arrested and imprisoned. Many were massacred, while the rest were transported in caravans to Marrakesh (Morocco). Timbuktu never fully recovered from the Moroccan invasion and its status and prestige as a major cultural, learning and trading centre eroded over time. The city continued to decline until 1893, when it was finally occupied by the French. In fact, most black scholars including Diop and Williams, believe that West Africa's intellectual heritage was largely lost after 1591.

Timbuktu became part of the newly independent Republic of Mali in 1960 and was designated a UNESCO World Heritage site in 1988.

Timbuktu is currently dealing with a number of challenges, including regional armed conflict, the destruction of its cultural heritage sites and the effects of desertification. As a result, UNESCO has added Timbuktu to its lists of endangered World Heritage sites. Nonetheless, the magnificence of this once-great city was declared in a 15th century West African proverb: "Salt comes from the north, Gold from the south, Silver from the land of white men, but the word of God and the treasures of wisdom come from Timbuktu."

UHURU

Uhuru (OO-hoo-roo) is the Swahili word for freedom or liberty. Swahili (aka Kiswahili) is a Bantu language that developed through trade between the coastal people of East Africa (from Somalia to Mozambique) and Arabs. It is the most widely spoken language in nearly a third of Africa, including Kenya, Tanzania, Uganda and parts of Congo. During the 1960s, the word *Uhuru* gained popularity and became a recognised slogan for all people of African descent worldwide in their struggle for independence, justice and equality. Uhuru is also the name of a well-known Pan-African movement founded in the US in 1972, under the leadership of Omali Yeshitela (born Joseph Waller on October 9, 1941). The goal of the movement is to unite black people of African descent from all across the world.

The term Uhuru is also associated with a symbolic landmark monument in Tanzania (white obelisk with a replica of the Uhuru Torch mounted at its top), the highest summit of one of Mt Kilimanjaro's volcanic cones, Kibo and the first orbiting satellite dedicated to X-ray astronomy. Two famous personalities with the name Uhuru are the former Kenyan President Uhuru Kenyatta and Black Uhuru, one of Jamaica's most popular bands whose lyrics deal with liberation and independence. In 1985, Black Uhuru won the first Grammy Award for Best Reggae Album.

VILLAGE

An African village is a community where people who share similar traditions and beliefs live together. Most African villages are organised into compounds, with people living in extended family groups. Each village is led by a village headman or chief, who is assisted by a council of elders. Prior to the era of European colonisation of Africa, this institution of traditional leadership was the sole authority. Living in an authentic African village is thought to be therapeutic because it provides its inhabitants with peace, love, unity, oneness and simple living. Even though village life is simple, there is a strong connection to family, culture and heritage.

Furthermore, an African village has a strong sense of community, with everyone contributing to its success. The *village square* is one of the most important areas in a village. It is a gathering place for the community, a market and a place where people can meet to debate community issues, tell stories and participate in cultural activities. Typically, African villages promote the spirit of oneness, or Ubuntu (meaning, *I am because we are*), which brings people together, especially during difficult times. Although many Africans now live in towns and cities, they still maintain a strong cultural bond with their villages, which they view as the source of their identity and ancestral home.

CHAPTER 2

WARRIOR

Since ancient times, the African continent has produced many great warriors and brilliant strategists, the majority of whom came from warrior nations such as the Ashante, Berber, Fulani, Maasai, Mandinka, Oromo, Somali, Shona and Zulu. Cetshwayo (also known as Cetewayo) kaMpande (1826-1884), the Zulu King, was one such example. In 1879, he and his 20,000-man army defeated the British military at the battle of Isandlhwana in present-day South Africa. The Zulu victory humiliated the British army because they were outmanoeuvred, outwitted and outfought. Another example is Ethiopian's great emperor, Menelik II (1844-1913), who emerged from the Horn of Africa and led his army to a crushing defeat against the Italian army at the Battle of Adowa (Ethiopia) in 1896.

Nana Yaa Asantewaa (1840-1921), Queen Mother of the Asante Empire in modern-day Ghana, was another well-known warrior. From 1900 to 1901, she led the Ashante rebellion known as the Anglo-Asante War (aka War of the Golden Stool or Yaa Asantewaa War) against British colonialism and imperialism, before being captured and exiled to the Seychelles following a long and bitter battle. Despite her death in exile in 1921, her resistance and incredible bravery inspired future generations to fight against various forms of indignity and injustice. The story of Yaa Asantewaa and her quest to protect the Golden Stool (the symbol and soul of the Asante Kingdom) shows "clearly that African women are not docile subjects waiting to be saved by the West; rather, they have collective agency and the power to challenge patriarchal practices in Africa" (Mensah, 2010, p.84; cited in Nyamekye, 2022). In Ghana, she is regarded as the heroine of feminism and is remembered for being the first African woman to lead a major war.

There is irrefutable evidence that Europeans did not completely dominate Africans militarily, as some argue. This was especially true for many powerful and well-organised states throughout Africa. They defended their territories until most were defeated and colonised by Europeans in the late 1800s. Other prominent African worthy of mentioning in the resistance of foreign incursion on their land, especially after colonisation was achieved, included the Agojie, female warriors from the kingdom of Dahomey (Republic of Benin), Samory Toure (Guinea), Amilcar Cabral (Guinea-Bissau), Patrice Lumumba (DRC), Kwame Nkrumah (Ghana), Steve Biko (South Africa), Thomas Sankara (Burkina Faso), Hendrik Witbooi (Namibia), Lock Priso (Cameroun), Almamy Suluku (Biriwa Kingdom, Sierra Leone), Oba (King) Ewuare Ogidigan of Benin Kingdom (Nigeria), Shaka Zulu (South Africa) and King Jaja of Opobo (Nigeria). The courage of these remarkable warrior leaders, demonstrated that colonial rule was strongly opposed. They are celebrated as heroes by their own people and the legacy they left behind is still felt around the world.

XYLOPHONE

The xylophone (which translates to *wood and sound*) is one of the world's oldest musical instruments, with reports of widespread use in Africa and Asia. However, "there is no evidence to prove the exact location of its first occurrence" (Gordon, 2020). The African xylophone is a type of wooden percussion instrument with deep cultural roots in Africa. Playing the xylophone involves hitting the wooden bars or keys with mallets and each bar produces a distinct set of sounds. Skilled players can produce complex melodies and rhythms, making it an adaptable instrument for both solo and ensemble performances. Mallet heads are typically made of rubber or leather.

Although xylophones can be found all over Africa, they are "most abundant in West, Eastern, Southern and are also common in Central Africa" (Hogan, 2014, as cited in Gordon, 2020). According to oral history, the xylophone was first documented in Africa in the 13th century, during the height of the ancient Mali Empire. This type of African xylophone, known as the *balafon*, is popular across West African. To resonate or amplify the sound, gourds (usually made of calabash) are cut to size and placed beneath the individually tuned wooden bars. The balafon is associated with the Griot profession (praise singers/oral historians), a long-established West African musical tradition that is still an important part of the region's cultural identity.

The xylophone was first introduced to Central America in the 16th century. The instrument was thought to have been brought by enslaved Africans during the trans-Atlantic slave trade (or through pre-Columbian African contact), as it resembled an African xylophone in both turning and construction. This xylophone, aka *Marimba*, can be found in parts of South America, several regions of Mexico and throughout Central America. The term marimba comes from the Bantu (African) language and is one of the many African names for the xylophone, particularly in Central, East and Southern Africa (Rager, 2008). This multipurpose instrument "has become so much a part of the culture and life of the peoples of Central America and South-eastern Mexico," (Garfias, 1983) and it is officially recognised as Guatemala's national instrument.

African xylophones are classified into two types: fixed bars and loose bars. Fixed bar are securely attached to one another, with resonators beneath them, whereas loose bars are arranged independently, with no resonators. The sound produced by xylophones with turned resonators is determined by the type of mallet used. Soft mallets produce lower tones, while hard mallets produce higher tones. Despite its unknown origins, the African xylophone boasts an incredible range and sound quality. Even as new musical instruments emerge, the ancient African instrument remains popular.

YAM

Yam (Dioscorea spp.) is a versatile vegetable and one of Africa's most widely consumed foods. There are several yam species, each with its own unique taste, appearance and size. Guinea yams are the most common yams grown in West Africa and they come in both white and yellow varieties. In fact, the West African region where yam was first domesticated around 5000 BCE (Andres, Adeoluwa & Bhullar, 2016) is known as the *yam belt* and it accounts for more than 90% of the world's yam crop, with Nigeria leading the way. This edible root crop or tuber can grow for six to ten months, depending on the species and then go dormant for two to four months. The growth and dormant periods are strongly related to the wet and dry seasons. At the start of the dry season, the yam begins to show signs of dormancy, indicating that it is ready for harvest. Yams can be cooked and eaten in a number of ways, including boiling, frying, roasting and baking. Furthermore, yams are high in carbohydrates and vitamin C, which can help fight colds and the flu. These tubers also contain calcium, iron, magnesium, potassium and phosphorus.

The word *yam* comes from two West African words, Nyam (Wolof) and Nyami (Fulani), both of which mean *to eat*. Yam is more than just

CHAPTER 2

8. Collage 2 (L-R)
Lemurs of Madagascar, Oware Board Game, The soul and spirit of the Asante nation lives in the Golding Stool, A section of the ruins of Great Zimbabwe

a traditional staple food for some African societies, as it's "ownership and cultivation have many cultural, religious and social meanings" (Obidiegwu & Akpabio 2017). For example, in pre-colonial Igbo culture, yams were associated with wealth and prosperity. The number of yam tubers a man owns indicates his level of influence in the community. Its use as a ritual object in many Igbo religious ceremonies is well documented (Nwoye, 2011). Several communities in West Africa and other African regions hold annual yam festivals to commemorate this root crop. Some of West Africa's well-known yam festivals include the Asogli Yam Festival (Te Za) in Ghana's Volta Region, the New Yam Festival (Iwa ji) of the Igbo people in Nigeria and the Benin Yam Festival (Tevi-hwé) among the Mahi people of

Savalou in the Republic of Benin. These yam festivals mark the end of one farming season and the start of another. They are frequently held on different dates in various communities between late July and October, attracting both locals and visitors. Many of these ethnic groups eat yam not only for its nutritional value, but also as a traditional symbolism deeply rooted in their culture.

ZIMBABWE

Zimbabwe is a wealthy and culturally diverse country in southern Africa. It shares borders with Botswana, Zambia, Mozambique and South Africa. This magnificent country's history dates back more than 5000 years to the Khoisan people. However, the earliest archaeological evidence of human settlements in the area dates back approximately 100,000 years ("Zimbabwe," 2011). There were great kingdoms and city-states in what is now Zimbabwe. However, many of these were crushed when the scramble for Africa began and the region eventually became a British colony known as Southern Rhodesia. In 1965, the white minority government declared independence and established the state of Rhodesia. The decision to break away from Britain was to avoid being ruled by an African majority.

After a long-period of colonial rule and 15 years of civil war, Zimbabwe gained independence from the United Kingdom in April 1980. It was named after Great Zimbabwe, the ancient stone city that was the capital of the Kingdom of Zimbabwe. At its peak, it had an estimated population of 20,000 people. The name 'Zimbabwe' is derived from the Shona words *dzimba dza mabwe*, meaning *houses of stone*. The magnificent stone sculptures that adorn this historical site were built without mortar and in stages between the 11th and

15th centuries. This feat of engineering demonstrates the skill and ingenuity of its builders. Zimbabwe's rulers are thought to have brought artistic and stone masonry traditions from the Kingdom of Mapungubwe, which began to fall around 1300 CE. Ironically, 19th century European colonialists attempted to rewrite history by claiming that the stonework at Great Zimbabwe was created by a lost white ancient civilisation rather than indigenous Africans, thereby undermining Africa's contribution to world heritage. In fact, several of Great Zimbabwe's monoliths align with specific bright stars in the constellation Orion as they rise on the morning of the winter solstice, the shortest day of the year. In terms of monumentality, the Great Zimbabwe ruins rank second only to the Egyptian pyramids of ancient Africa. Zimbabwe today is home to numerous national parks and Africa's largest waterfall, the magnificent Victoria Falls (known locally as the Smoke that Thunders).

9. Collage 3 (L-R)

Saharan rock painting, Vintage Nigerian stamp honouring Queen Amina of Zaria, Rhinos at a game park in Southern Africa, African Zulu Warrior

Chapter 3

CONCLUSION

To summarise, Africa is the place where humanity originated. This continent, once called the *Dark Continent*, has been filled with light ever since the arrival of the first human ancestor. Without exaggeration, Africa is the reason why everything exists, and this book debunks the false narrative spread by Europeans and others that the African continent made no contribution to civilisation. Africa, like a palm tree swaying in a storm but not breaking, has weathered the terrible, brutal blows of slavery and colonialism. These experiences raise the question of whether Africa requires a renaissance to reclaim much of what has been lost over centuries of foreign invasions. Many of its sovereign states have made some progress since gaining independence from their former colonial rulers, but much more work is needed, particularly breaking free from neo-colonial legacies that still dominates the continent.

Despite the dominant media's negative portrayal of Africa, the continent and its people are making significant progress in every imaginable area. Africans are resilient people who must learn to utilise their vast resources to achieve greater heights. According to the evidence presented in this book, Africa has the potential to redefine and strengthen its role in the international community. As many African countries look to the future, they must consider how to deal with the challenges posed by the fourth and fifth industrial revolutions, aka the age of digital colonialism, as well as the transhumanism agenda (human-machine collaboration). They should also be prepared to deal decisively with Western policies that may seek to undermine or threaten their values, beliefs, norms, philosophies, dressing and overall way of life. This is not scaremongering; the negative effects of globalisation have already started.

Ultimately, Africans must recognise that they are still dealing with the descendants of those who plundered their resources for centuries, rewrote their history, enslaved millions of their people and colonised almost all of their lands. These *globalists*, as they are now known, could be individuals or organisations who are only interested in advancing themselves at the expense of the vast majority of people. Furthermore, Africans should be open to questioning and challenging any aspect of their history that others may have passed down to them. Many of these are believed to carry negative connotations. In today's complex world, Africans on the continent and in the diaspora should pay close attention to the potential outcomes of the various global crisis that have occurred since 2020, as there has been talk of reimaging and resetting the world. Therefore, it is critical that they remain informed about these developments, understand their implications, participate in discussions as needed and make their voices heard. They must also remember that many of their ancestors fought against injustice, exploitation and oppression, and that history has a way of repeating itself, especially for those who refuse to learn from it. Nonetheless, all indicators point to Africa having a bright future.

THE WAY FORWARD FOR AFRICA

In going forward, Africa must consider taking the following steps to finally gain the recognition it so richly deserves:

☼ Have a new generation of decisive leaders with integrity, a clear vision for the future and a willingness to defend and improve both their own countries and the African continent. This preferred leadership must be fearless and ready to confront the global order head on. To bring such leaders to power, African countries must have effective processes in place, such as an honest and fair electoral and judicial system. Citizens in these countries must also understand their right to hold elected government officials and their institutions accountable.

☼ Abandon the failed European governance model left behind by colonial Europe in favour of one that considers both people's needs and the distinct characteristics of each African country. To accelerate Africa's industrial development, each of its 54 countries must create a model tailored to its specific needs, taking into account cultural, economic, environmental and social diversity, rather than simply adopting a Western or East Asian model. They must refuse to allow Western institutions like the WTO, IMF and World Bank to impose their economic models at the expense of their own citizens.

☼   African leaders must limit foreign intervention, strengthen local capacity and create an environment in which Africans can shape their own narratives and destiny. In addition, they should stop transplanting foreign solutions to Africa and instead rely on local talent to solve many of the continent's problems. Even though, achieving progress is the goal, these leaders must address Africa's massive brain drain, promote good governance, eradicate gross corruption and multi-dimensional poverty, build a self-sufficient, successful and resilient Africa, and proceed with extreme caution when dealing with the issue of globalisation.

☼   Africa will benefit from studying its pre-colonial history, as well as the political and ideological resources that supported successful African civilisations such as ancient Egypt, Ghana, Mali, Songhai and many others. Identifying and implementing the most effective policies will serve as a springboard for the modernisation, integration and revitalisation of many African countries. This will usher in a new Africa, one that is far more powerful and beneficial to the entire world, while also instilling in its people a sense of collective pride and true sovereignty.

☼   The paternal relationship that developed between Africa and the West during colonial rule must be replaced by a long-term, sustainable relationship in which both parties are treated equally. In terms of resource management, African leaders should hire skilled negotiators, preferably from the continent or diaspora. During negotiations, representatives from any African country should be more assertive and well-prepared with relevant data, including knowledge of production, reserves, quantities and production volumes, to ensure that they get the most out of their resources. They should never rely on information from the other side, as has always been the case. Moreover, they should set and control the prices of their own resources, rather than leave it to the western-controlled financial markets.

☼ African leaders should continue to advocate for reforms to several international institutions, including the IMF, World Bank, WHO, WTO and the composition of the United Nations Security Council (UNSC). All of these organisations are part of a colonial construct that existed before African countries gained independence. As a result, African leaders, through the African Union, must not allow the West to dictate how these organisations are reformed, such as the United States' support for Africa to have two permanent seats on the UNSC with *no veto power*, which was announced on September 12, 2024. Their proposal is to withhold veto power from Africa's proposed two seats, despite the fact that the five original permanent members, the United States, the United Kingdom, France, China and Russia, have always had veto power. This demonstrates how Africa is still not treated equally.

☼ Governments throughout Africa should keep track of the *developmental work* of international NGOs and local partners operating in their communities. This is significant because the development role played by these NGOs continues to reflect the old imperialistic nature and colonial habits of missionaries and voluntary organisations that contributed to Europe's colonisation and control of Africa. Despite their increasing numbers and significant funding, they have yet to address many of Africa's development challenges.

☼ The African Union must pursue a Pan-African agenda that unifies all member states, including the diaspora, which it refers to as its 6th region. This is required to promote African solidarity and advance the goals of an African Renaissance. Whenever possible, they should recruit the best and brightest minds from either the continent or the diaspora. Each member state will then be expected to assist in the integration of successful candidates into all aspects of development policy and nation-building. This strategy will ensure that Africa is rebuilt by its own people, rather than those with vested interests elsewhere.

☀ In terms of education, African leaders must maintain their cultural identities. They must ensure that African culture, history, customs, and the many indigenous languages are preserved, promoted and taught in educational institutions and curriculums. This is necessary to keep one's identity as an African because a people without identity are without roots, and a person without roots is devoid of life. These requirements are essential to honour the ancestors and extract values for Africa's renaissance.

☀ On the issue of climate change, Africa is under pressure to increase spending to reduce carbon emissions and avoid the worst of the problem, despite the fact that African countries account for only about 4% of total global emissions. African leaders, particularly those from poorer countries, must prioritise their most basic needs in order to improve the lives of their citizens. Most cannot afford the funds needed to mitigate climate change, and are still obligated to repay their existing debts to global financial institutions. Overextending themselves will almost certainly slow their economic growth. To prevent the catastrophic effects of climate change, they must ask Western countries and other historically significant polluters to contribute more to the cost of climate change.

"To control a people you must first control what they think about themselves and how they regard their history and culture. And when your conqueror makes you ashamed of your culture and your history, he needs no prison walls and no chains to hold you."

- JOHN HENRIK CLARKE (1915-1998)

"When we get a strong Africa, the person of African origin or African ancestry will be respected any place on this earth."

- MALCOLM X (1925-1965)

AFRICAN PROVERBS
Wisdom from Africa

African proverbs are short, memorable and understandable sayings that usually contain words of wisdom, truths, or morals based on common sense or practical experience. They reflect the cultural values, beliefs and wisdom of African societies, providing insight into their history, customs and way of life, and were passed down through African ancestors from generation to generation.

Furthermore, African proverbs are more than just about culture or traditions; they demonstrate that wisdom comes from the everyday experiences and stories shared by people over time, not just from books or technology. These *words of wisdom* are still spoken throughout Africa and contain many valuable life lessons.

NYANSAPO (Wisdom Knot) is an Adinkra symbol.
It represents wisdom, ingenuity, intelligence and patience.

INSPIRATIONAL AFRICAN PROVERBS AND THEIR MEANING

1. Do not point to the ruins of your father's house with your left hand.
   Meaning: *Do not scorn culture inherited from your ancestors.*

2. Wisdom is like a baobab tree; no one individual can embrace it.
   Meaning: *True wisdom is vast and multifaceted, requiring the collective understanding and contributions of many people.*

3. The child who is not embraced by the village will burn it down to feel its warmth.
   Meaning: *Neglect and isolation can lead to destructive behaviour as a means of seeking attention and care.*

4. Even if the cock does not crow, the sun will rise.
   Meaning: *What is meant to be will be.*

5. The battle of grasshoppers is a feast for the hawks.
   Meaning: *If you are not united, you open doors for attacks.*

6. The rain does not fall on one roof alone.
   Meaning: *Challenges and hardships are a universal part of life and affect everyone.*

7. However long the night, the dawn will break.
   Meaning: *No matter how difficult or demanding the challenge, there is always hope for a better tomorrow.*

8. A single bracelet does not jingle.
   Meaning: *You can't succeed on your own; you need collaboration and support.*

9. The best way to fight an alien and oppressive culture is to embrace your own.
   Meaning: *The best way to drive out darkness is to turn on the light.*

10. What an old man sees from the ground, a boy cannot see even if he stands on top of the mountain.
    Meaning: *True wisdom is gained only through experience and years of self-reflection.*

11. When elephants fight, it's the grass that suffers.
    Meaning: *When people in positions of power fight to satisfy their own egos, it's the general population that suffers the most.*

12. A roaring lion kills no game.
    Meaning: *Focus your energy not on talking/bragging or trying to impress others, but on quietly working towards your goals. Let the results of your actions speak for themselves.*

13. A smooth sea never made a skillful sailor.
    Meaning: *It's the obstacles and failures in your life that lead you to new insights, make you more knowledgeable and skillful.*

14. If you wish to move mountains tomorrow, you must start by lifting stones today.
    Meaning: *Focus on the small things or what needs to be done at this moment and slowly but surely you will be able to achieve big results.*

15. Only a fool tests the depth of water with both feet.
    Meaning: *Always test a situation or venture by starting small and learning the ins and outs before fully investing in it.*

GLOSSARY

African Union   *The African Union* is a continental body made up of 55 Member States that represent all countries on the African continent. It was officially established in 2002 as the successor to the Organisation of African Unity (OAU, 1963-1999).

AKA   Also Known As.

Ancient Ghana   *Ancient Ghana* and the modern country of Ghana are not the same. The leaders of present-day Ghana chose this as the name for their country because the empire of ancient Ghana had been so great. In fact, the word Ghana means "warrior-king" and was the title of the Kings of Wagadu.

BCE   *BCE* stands for "before the common/current era". (Formerly BC)

CE   *CE* stands for "common /current) era". (Formerly AD)

Colonialism   *Colonialism* refers to the establishment of a colony in one territory by a political power from another territory.

Globalisation   *Globalisation* is the process by which economies and cultures are drawn closer together and become more interconnected via global trade networks, capital flows, and the spread of technology and global media.

Kemet/KMT *Kemet/KMT* is the name given to Egypt by its ancient indigenous people. It translates literally as 'the black land' or 'land of the blacks.'

Neo-colonialism *Neo-colonialism* is the practice of using capitalism, globalisation, cultural imperialism, and conditional aid to exert influence over a developing country rather than the traditional colonial methods of direct military or indirect political control.

Nomarchs *Nomarchs* in Ancient Egypt were essentially regional/provincial governors who presided over districts of Egypt in the absence of a Pharaoh.

Pharmacopoeia *Pharmacopoeia* is an official book that lists all the drugs [plants and other substances] that can be used to treat people in a particular country [region], and describes how to [prepare] and use them.

Population density Population density measures how densely populated an area is. It is calculated by dividing the total population of a region by the total land area.

Western World *Western World*, or simply the West: Europe, North America and generally any country whose cultural and ethnic origins can mostly be traced to Europe such as Australia and New Zealand.

BIBLIOGRAPHY

1. Adam, J. (2022) Slavery and the bank. City of London. London. [17 January 2024].

2. Adojoh, A.A. (2020). "A Study of Igala Origin: An Evidence-Based Approach." International Journal of Trend in Research and Development, 7(4), 250-254.

3. Adaki, A.Y. (2023). "The Role of Westernization in the Changing African Family Structures: A Systematic Literature Review." Humanities, Society and Community. 1 (1), 60-73. https://doi.org/10.31098/hsc.v1i1.1795

4. 'African Elephant' (n.d.) World Wildlife Fund (W.W.F). Retrieved from: https://www.worldwildlife.org/species/african-elephant [Accessed: 2 January, 2024].

5. Andindilile, M. (2016). "You have no past, no history: Philosophy, literature and the re-invention of Africa." International Journal of English and Literature. 7 (8), 127-134. DOI: 10.5897/IJEL2015.0729

6. Andres C., Adeoluwa O. O., Bhullar G. S. (2017). "Yam (*Dioscorea* spp.)." In Thomas B., Murray B. G., Murphy D. J, (Eds). Encyclopedia of Applied Plant Sciences, Vol. 3, Waltham, MA: Academic Press, 435-441.

7. Antwi-Baffour, S. et al. (2014). "The Place of Traditional Medicine in the African Society: The Science, Acceptance and Support." American Journal of Health Research. 2 (2), 49-54. Doi: 10.11648/j.ajhr.20140202.13

8. Ba, D. (2007). Africans still seething over Sarkozy speech. Reuters. Retrieved from: https://www.reuters.com/article/idUSL05130346/

9. Bamalli, Z. et al. (2014). "Baobab Tree (Adansonia digitata L) Parts: Nutrition, Applications in Food and Uses in Ethno-medicine - A Review."

Annals of Nutritional Disorders & Therapy. 1(3), 1011

10. Bennett, A. (2019). "Material Cultures of Imperialism in Eastern Africa, c.1870-1920: A Study of Ethnographic Collecting and Display." Doctoral thesis (Ph.D.), UCL (University College London).

11. Ben Yedder, O. (2024). "We need to counter negative stereotypes and uplift Africa's image in the world." African Business. Retrieved from: https://african.business/2024/05/african-banker/we-need-to-counter-negative-stereotypes-and-uplift-africas-image-in-the-world-adesina. [Accessed: 7 August, 2024].

12. Bayeck, Rebecca Y. (2018). "African board games should be introduced into the classroom." Quartz Africa Weekly. Retrieved from: https://qz.com/africa/1174530/african-board-games-like-oware-moruba-and-mancala-should-be-included-in-school/

13. Benyera, E. (2021). The Fourth Industrial Revolution and the Recolonisation of Africa: The Coloniality of Data (1st Ed.). Routledge: London

14. Brown, K. (2018). "Benin's Looted Bronzes Are All Over the Western World. Here Are 7 Museums That Hold Over 2,000 of the Famed Sculptures." ArtNet News. Retrieved from: https://news.artnet.com/art-world/benin-bronzes-restitution-1322807

15. Campbell, G. (2016). "Malagasy empires (Sakalava and Merina)." In: MacKenzie, J.M. (ed.). The Encyclopedia of Empire (1st ed., pp. 1-6). John Wiley & Sons, Ltd. https://doi.org/10.1002/9781118455074.wbeoe056

16. Charles, E. A. (1977). Precolonial Senegal: the Jolof Kingdom, 1800-1890. Boston: African Studies Center, Boston University.

17. Chang'ach, J.K. (2015). "If Ancient Egyptians were Negroes, then European Civilization is but a Derivation of African Achievements." Arts and Social Sciences Journal, 6: 098, DOI: 10.4172/2151-6200.1000098.

18. Chu, J. (2013). "A *green* Sahara was far less dusty than today," MIT News. April 5, 2013. Retrieved from: https://news.mit.edu/2013/sahara-was-far-less-dusty-than-today-0405

19. Connor, S. (2003). "The world's oldest humans: proof we came from Africa." The Independent. Retrieved from: https://www.independent.co.uk/news/science/the-worlds-oldest-humans-proof-we-came-from-africa-108530.html

20. Curtis, M. and Jones, T. (2017). "Honest Accounts 2017: How the World Profits from Africa's Wealth." Global Justice Now: London, UK. Retrieved from: https://jubileedebt.org.uk/wp-content/uploads/2017/05/Honest-Accounts-2017-WEB-FINAL.pdf

21. Diop, C.A. (1974). The African origin of civilization: Myth or reality. Chicago, IL: Lawrence Hill & Company.

22. DNA Tribes Digest (2012). Genetic Analysis of Amarna Mummies. Retrieved from: https://thednatests.com/dnatribes-digest-2012-01-01.pdf

23. Eurogroup for animals. (2022). 136 NGOs around the world call for a ban on hunting trophy imports. Retrieved from: https://www.eurogroupforanimals.org/news/136-ngos-around-world-call-ban-hunting-trophy-imports [Accessed November 15, 2023].

24. Fuller, H. (2009). "From Cowries to Coins: Money and Colonialism in the Gold Coast and British West Africa in the Early 20th Century," in Money in Africa, ed. Catherine Eagleton, Harcourt Fuller, and John Perkins, 54-61. London: British Museum Research Publications.

25. Garfias, R. (1983). "The Marimba of Mexico and Central America." Latin American Music Review/Revista de Musica Latinoamericana, 4(2), pp. 203-228. Doi: 10.2307/780267

26. Gordon, G.A. (2020) "Marimbas in South African schools: gateway instruments for the Indigenous African Music curriculum." [Masters Dissertation, Stellenbosch University] Stellenbosch University. Retrieved from: https://scholar.sun.ac.za/handle/10019.1/109090

27. Hadero, H. (2019). "How Jollof rice became West Africa's iconic dish and a point of banter between Africans." Retrieve from: https://qz.com/africa/1689421/the-history-of-jollof-rice-in-west-africa-and-the-banter

28. Harris, J. and Wente, E. (1980). An x-ray atlas of the royal mummies. Chicago: University of Chicago Press.

29. Haour, A. et al. (2016). "Tracking the Cowrie Shell: Excavations in the Maldives." Nyame Akuma, 85, 69-77. Retrieved from: https://core.ac.uk/download/pdf/157817156.pdf

30. 'King Cetshwayo.' (2011). South Africa's History Online (S.A.H.O.). Retrieved from: https://www.sahistory.org.za/people/king-cetshwayo

31. Krzyszkowska, O. and Morkot, R. (2000). Ivory and related materials. In: Nicholson, P.T. and Shaw, I, (Eds). Ancient Egyptian Materials and Technology. Cambridge, UK: Cambridge University Press, 320-331.

32. Koutonin, M. (2016). "Isn't it Europe that is overpopulated, rather than Africa?" Retrieved from https://www.theguardian.com/global-development-professionals-network/2016/jan/11/europe-africa-overpopulated-global-population [Accessed November 21, 2023].

33. Leader-Williams, N. (1992). The world trade in rhino horn: A review. Cambridge, UK: Traffic International.

34. Lemieux, A. M., & Clarke, R. V. (2009). "The international ban on ivory sales and its effects on elephant poaching in Africa." British Journal of Criminology, 49(4), 451-471. https://doi.org/10.1093/bjc/azp030

35. Lindsaya, K. et al. (2017). "The shared nature of Africa's elephants." Biological Conservation, 215, 260-267. Retrieved from: http://dx.doi.org/10.1016/j.biocon.2017.08.021

36. Mafumbate, R. (2019). "The undiluted African community: Values, the family, orphanage and wellness in traditional Africa." In Information and Knowledge Management 9 (8), 7-13.

37. Mahomoodally, F.M. (2013). "Traditional Medicines in Africa: An Appraisal of Ten Potent African Medicinal Plants." Evidence-Based Complementary and Alternative Medicine. Retrieved from: http://dx.doi.org/10.1155/2013/617459

38. Mamba, H. S. (2018). "Human and Climate Change Influences on Black (Diceros bicornis) and White (Ceratotherium simum) Rhinos in Southern Africa." [Masters Dissertation, University of Massachusetts Amherst].

39. Maweu, J.M. (2011). "Indigenous ecological knowledge and modern western ecological knowledge. Complimentary, not contradictory. Thought and Practice." A Journal of the Philosophical Association of Kenya 3(2), 35-47.

40. Mokhtar, G. (Ed.). (1990). General History of Africa, Vol. II, Ancient Civilizations of Africa. London: James Currey Publishers.

41. Mote, P.W. & Kaser, G. (2007). "The shrinking glaciers of Kilimanjaro: Can global warming be blamed?" American Scientist 95(4): 318-325. Retrieved from: https://www.americanscientist.org/article/the-shrinking-glaciers-of-kilimanjaro-can-global-warming-be-blamed [Accessed 6 February 2024].

42. Msindo, E. (2019, 17-19 July). "Writing history beyond Trevor-Roper: The Experience of African History, with special reference to Zimbabwe." [Keynote Speech]. Zimbabwe Historical Association. Rhodes University, South Africa.

43. Nkrumah, K. (1974). Africa Must Unite. London: Panaf Books Ltd.

44. Nwoye, C. M. A. (2011). "Igbo cultural and religious worldview: An insider's perspective." International Journal of Sociology and Anthropology 3(9), 304-317. http://www.academicjournals.org/IJSA

45. Nyamekye, R. (2022). "Unseating Broken Stories: A Decolonizing Case Study of Warrior Queenmother, Nana Yaa Asantewaa." [Doctoral dissertation, University of Saskatchewan].

46. Obidiegwu, J.E., Akpabio, E.M. (2017). "The geography of yam cultivation in Southern Nigeria: Exploring its social meanings and cultural functions." Journal of Ethnic Foods, 4:28-35. https://doi.org/10.1016/j.jef.2017.02.004

47. Odunbaku, B. (2012). "Importance of cowrie shells in pre-colonial Yoruba land Southwestern Nigeria: Orile-Keesi as a case study." International Journal of Humanities and Social Science 2(18): 234-241.

48. Olusegun, O. (2015). "Yoruba indigenous drums: An aesthetic symbol in ecological ritual of the Yoruba people." European Scientific Journal, ESJ, 11(5). Retrieved from: https://eujournal.org/index.php/esj/article/view/5186

49. 'Oware rules' (n.d.). The Oware Society. Retrieved from: http://www.oware.org/rules.asp [Accessed 8 January 2024].

50. Patrut, A. et al. (2018). "The demise of the largest and oldest African baobabs." Nature Plants 4: 423-426. DOI: 10.1038/s41477-018-0170-5.

51. Pedersen, Traci. (2016). "The Nile: Longest River in the World." Live Science. Retrieved from: https://www.livescience.com/57023-nile-river-facts.html

52. Perry, P. (2022). Black or white? Ancient Egyptian race mystery now solved: A study describes how researchers conducted the first successful DNA sequencing on ancient Egyptian mummies. Retrieved from: https://bigthink.com/surprising-science/were-the-ancient-egyptians-black-or-white-scientists-now-know/

53. Rager, D. (2008). "The History of the Marimba." Music Faculty Publications. 1. http://engagedscholarship.csuohio.edu/clmusic_facpub/1

54. Rodland, H. (2021). "Swahili social landscapes: Material expressions of identity, agency, and labour in Zanzibar, 1000–1400 CE." Uppsala University.

55. Rothman, N. C. (2002). "Indian Ocean trading links: The Swahili experience." Comparative Civilizations Review, 46 (46), 1–13.Google Scholar

56. Schuenemann, V. J. et al. (2017). "Ancient Egyptian mummy genomes suggest an increase of Sub-Saharan African ancestry in post-Roman periods." Nature Communication. 8: 15694. Retrieved from: https://doi.org/10.1038/ncomms15694

57. Schulz, N. (2020). "The politics of export restrictions: a panel data analysis of African commodity processing industries." World development, Vol. 130. Retrieved from: http://eprints.lse.ac.uk/103779/

58. Shizha, E. and Charema, J. (2011). "Health and wellness in Southern Africa: Incorporating indigenous and western healing practices." International Journal of Psychology and Counselling, 3(9), 167-175.

59. Shuriye, A.O. and Ibrahim, D.S. (2013). "Timbuktu Civilization and its Significance in Islamic History." Mediterranean Journal of Social Sciences, 4(11), 696-704. Doi:10.5901/mjss.2013.v4n11p696

60. Stoffle, R. W. et al. (2016) "The Name of the Game: Oware men's social space during Caribbean Slavery to Post-Colonial Times." International Journal of Intangible Heritage, 11, 75-99.

61. Team A.G. (2021). "How the Kilimanjaro glaciers left truth in the cold." Retrieved from: https://africageographic.com/stories/how-the-kilimanjaro-glaciers-left-truth-in-the-cold/ [Accessed 6 February 2024].

62. Teeter, E. (2011). Before the Pyramids: The Origins of Egyptian Civilization. Chicago, Illinois: Oriental Institute of the University of Chicago. Retrieved from: https://oi-idb-static.uchicago.edu/multimedia/88/oimp33.pdf

63. Taringa, N.T. (n.d.). The Sacred Duty of Animals in African Traditional Religion and Culture. "Future Africa": Appropriating Natures for the Future: Africa and Beyond. https://www.bayreuth-academy-futureafrica.uni-bayreuth.de/resources/WG-C_Taringa_Animals-in-African-Traditional-Religion.pdf [Accessed: 2nd July, 2024].

64. Thevet, A. (1575). Cosmographie Universelle. Vol.2. Paris: l'Huillier.

65. Vigne L, and Martin E. (2018). "Illegal rhino horn trade in eastern Asia still threatens Kruger's rhinos." The Aspinall Foundation, UK.

66. Volney, M. C-F. (1787). Travels through Syria and Egypt in the Years 1783, 1784, and 1785, vol 1, p. 80-83. London: G. G. J. and J. Robinson.

67. Watterson, C. (2008). "The development of African history as a discipline in the English-speaking world: a study of academic infrastructure." Master's thesis (MA), Victoria University of Wellington.

68. West, P. M. (2005). "The lion's mane: neither a token of royalty nor a shield for fighting, the mane is a signal of quality to mates and rivals, but one that comes with consequences." American Scientist, 93(3), 226-235. Retrieved from: https://www.uvm.edu/~dstratto/bcor102/LionsMane.pdf

69. Yang, B. (2019) Cowrie Shells and Cowrie Money: A Global History. London. Routledge.

70. 'Zimbabwe' (2011) South Africa's History Online (S.A.H.O). Retrieved from: https://www.sahistory.org.za/place/zimbabwe [Accessed: 2 January, 2024].

Thank you to all the many online websites that were visited but not listed while researching materials for the book.

RECOMMENDED READING

1. Conrad, D. (2005). Empires of Medieval West Africa: Ghana, Mali, and Songhay. New York: Facts on File.

2. Diop, C. A. (1987). Precolonial black Africa: A comparative study of the political and social systems of Europe and black Africa, from antiquity to the formation of modern states. Brooklyn, NY: Lawrence Hill Books.

3. Farrar, V.T. (2020). Precolonial African Material Culture: Combatting Stereotypes of Technological Backwardness. Lanham, Maryland: Lexington Books.

4. Gomez, Michael. (2018). African Dominion: A New History of Empire in Early and Medieval West Africa. Princeton, NJ: Princeton University Press.

5. James, G. G. M. (2010). Stolen legacy: The Egyptian origins of western philosophy. Almanor, CA: Feather Trail Press.

6. MacKenzie, J. M. (1983). The Partition of Africa, 1880-1900 and European Imperialism in the 19th Century. London and New York: Methuen.

7. Sweetman, David (1984). Women Leaders in African History (African Historical Biographies. New York City, NY: Pearson Education Limited.

8. Van Sertima, Ivan. (1983). Blacks in Science: Ancient and Modern. (Journal of African Civilizations). New Brunswick, NJ: Transaction Books.

9. Van Sertima, Ivan. (1988). African Presence in Early America. New Jersey, NJ: Transaction Publishers.

10. Walker, R. (2006). When We Ruled: The ancient and Medieval History of Black Civilisation. London: Every Generation Media.

11. Walter, R. (1989). How Europe Undeveloped Africa. Nairobi: East African Educational Publishers.

12. William, C. (1987). The destruction of black civilisation: Great issues of a race from 4500 B.C. to 2000 A.D. Chicago, IL: Third World Press.

www.ingramcontent.com/pod-product-compliance
Lightning Source LLC
Chambersburg PA
CBHW030307100526
44590CB00012B/558